MW00440866

Mike Belkin:

Socks, Sports, Rock and Art

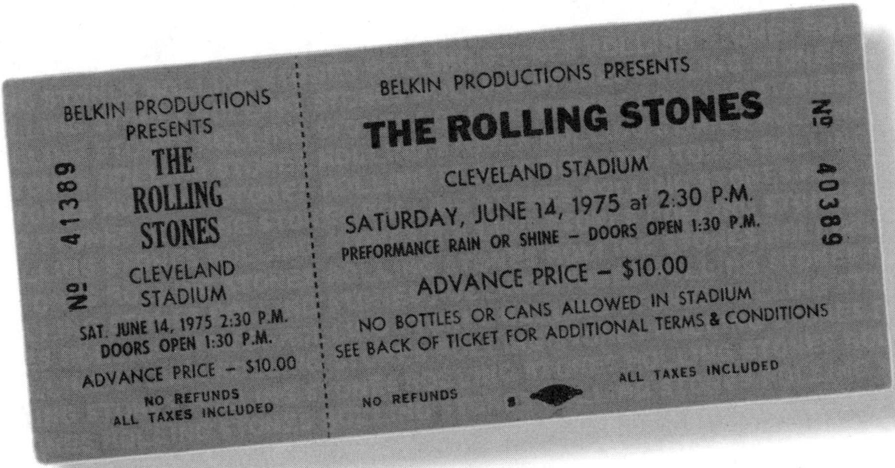

Also by Carlo Wolff

Cleveland Rock & Roll Memories

The Encyclopedia of Record Producers
(co-author)

Mike Belkin:

Socks, Sports, Rock and Art

Joe,
Enjoy this!

Carlo Wolff with Mike Belkin *That's*
ME
Illustrations by Ron Hill — *Ron*
Hill

Carlo Wolff

Act3

Mike Belkin: Socks, Sports, Rock and Art
by Carlo Wolff with Mike Belkin

Copyright © 2017 Mike Belkin

Book Design © 2017 Act 3 LLC

Cover and Interior Illustrations by Ron Hill
© 2017 Act 3 LLC

ISBN 978-1-5323-4517-3

October 2017
All rights reserved. No part of this book may be used or
reproduced in any manner whatsoever without written
permission from the publisher except in the case of
brief quotations embodied in critical articles or reviews.
For more information or inquiries, contact:
Act 3 LLC | 12200 Fairhill Road, Cleveland, OH 44120
+1 216 325 7777

Published by

www.Act3Creative.com

2nd Printing

I dedicate this book to the glory that
rock 'n' roll can be, to the imagination –
and to Mike Belkin.

Carlo Wolff

I dedicate this book to my family,
past and present –
My parents, Sam and Pola; and my four
wonderful, lovable aunts.
My wife Annie; my sons Michael and Sam,
and my daughter Lisa.

Mike Belkin

" I don't saddle up to come in second."

Mike Belkin

Contents

Introduction

by Frankie Valli

I've been to Cleveland too many times to count since the Four Seasons began playing there starting in the '60s; I still perform in Cleveland frequently. But I can't think of Cleveland without thinking of Mike Belkin, the guy who produced most of those early dates. Mike was always the most honorable and the most credible promoter on the road.

The two of us have a true friendship, something that's so rare in this business. I always look forward to working with Mike. We have broken bread together over six different decades. I remember when his kids were born. And I regret that we can't spend more time just reminiscing at his farmhouse in the country.

Frankie Valli still tours to this day. Here he is at a recent concert.

I'm eighty-three years old. I grew up in the projects, and thanks to lessons learned at the School of Hard Knocks, I've been very successful. But it's been a tough road, I've been up and down three or four times. All the way from success to broke, success to broke. This business is a tough go.

Through it all, I worked hard at not only my craft, but also at keeping my integrity; that is so important. There are so many untrustworthy people out there. As far as I'm concerned, when you shook a guy's hand, you had a deal. I'm still partners with Bob Gaudio, my partner as a performer, songwriter, and producer. Can you believe it? Fifty-five years on a handshake, and either one of us knows we can leave anytime we like. And that's because we trust each other—why would anyone work with someone they didn't trust and like? I find this approach makes it easier to go to sleep at night; and in the morning I can look in the mirror and not be ashamed of what I see.

And that's why Mike and I click. Mike can see through all the phoniness. You'll see that in this book of Mike's amazing life.

Everybody likes a winner. But Mike and I have been friends when I'm up, and when I'm down. He always used all his resources to promote my shows, whether we were doing terrific or not. It's those qualities and that integrity that I don't forget. I thank God, that if I ever need anything, I know I can call on Mike, and he'd be there. That's what life is all about.

Frankie Valli
Los Angeles, California
August 2017

Frankie Valli is one of the founding members of the Four Seasons. In 1999, the group was inducted into the Rock and Roll Hall of Fame in Cleveland, Ohio.

Warm-up Act

by Carlo Wolff

When I moved to Cleveland from Albany, New York, in 1986, I was eager to write about rock 'n' roll in a far larger market, especially one with a rich musical legacy. It didn't take long to learn that the area's key entertainment promoter was Belkin Productions. Soon afterward, I made an appointment to meet Mike Belkin and his older brother, Jules—and I felt the connection immediately. The two have always helped me out as a journalist. They also made me feel at home from the start.

It became clear that the Belkin brothers were instrumental in making Cleveland a rock 'n' roll breakout city. They sensed the direction of the music and the market, and then they rode a very lucrative and synergistic wave as their company's growth paralleled the rise of rock itself. In the process, Belkin Productions became the stuff of legend.

They were at the heart of it all as they presented the World Series of Rock shows in Cleveland; the Rubber Bowl shows in Akron: a record-breaking Rolling Stones date at the old Cleveland Municipal Stadium; the James Gang tours with The Who; and a four date, record-setting stand by the Michael Stanley Band (MSB). In addition, the Belkins also promoted or co-promoted numerous concerts throughout the Midwest and farther afield.

Of special significance to Mike are the James Gang, MSB, Donnie Iris and the Cruisers, and Wild Cherry. Belkin's involvement with these groups signaled his shift in focus to talent management in the early '70s as both brothers continued to run Belkin Productions. While the James Gang hasn't toured since 2006, Belkin still manages performers including Michael Stanley and Donnie Iris. Because of a record deal he set up with his buddy Carl Maduri, Belkin remains connected to Wild Cherry, whose signature recording "Play That Funky Music (White Boy)" has been called "the blackest song a white band ever recorded."

A multi-faceted promoter and businessman, Belkin also conceived and for 24 years produced the Great American Rib Cook-Off & Music Festival, four days of food and music in the Flats, Cleveland's riverside entertainment district.

Today, in his 80s, Belkin remains an active, hands-on guy. He is president of Pinnacle Marketing & Distribution, a sports merchandising firm he founded in 2001. That was the same year he and his brother sold Belkin Productions to Live Nation precursor SFX.

His oldest son, Michael, is now in charge of booking Live Nation events in Ohio, western Pennsylvania, West Virginia and Kentucky. Belkin, meanwhile, still works every day at one or both offices: Live Nation in Chagrin Falls and the Pinnacle office in Bedford Heights. And he and his son continue to run MB Management out of Chagrin Falls as well.

Belkin is active and contemporary, but at the same time he's old school. He still writes letters. A handshake counts for him. To Belkin, family is business and business is family.

While Michael Belkin steers Live Nation, Belkin and his wife, Annie, work together in both the sports marketing and merchandising business and in art. The couple are known as high-profile collectors of contemporary art glass. Their numerous donations of striking pieces have enhanced the collections of the Akron Art Museum, the Cleveland Museum of Art, and several other notable museums nationwide.

At Mike and Annie's home, art rules. While their collection of contemporary art attests to the couple's taste, the house's artwork and the striking furnishings are anything but ostentatious. Exquisitely detailed art glass by the flower-drunk Paul Stankard cohabits with a mannequin just learning the value of underwear.

Belkin also is a philanthropist and civic activist, as is his brother. The two were critical in making Cleveland the home of the Rock and Roll Hall of Fame.

Best known as a pioneer in the rock 'n' roll business, Mike Belkin is a man to whom family, blood and otherwise, means everything. He's a man of taste, and a hard-nosed businessman. He knows the value of networking, and prizes loyalty, straightforwardness and affection.

Belkin never has outgrown his inner scamp. He can be funny, even cutting. He also cries easily. And he's a patriot, regarding both the United States and Israel.

If the first floor of Mike and Annie's home is dedicated to entertainment, the ground floor, where Belkin works and hangs out, is the floor of knowledge. On your way down the narrow staircase, you'll pass gold and platinum records for Wild Cherry and the James Gang. You'll also see a photograph of a gigantic Stones concert—at least 83,000 attended on that sweltering July day in 1978.

Look, but don't touch. Above all, don't mess with the boxes on the floor that Belkin has amassed over the years. While they attest to his packrat tendencies—"I'm a hoarder," he admits—they help preserve and form the record of his life. The collection might be a little chaotic. But it's also priceless.

Those boxes are pure gold. Along with the ledger books and Rolodexes he kept so meticulously, you find keepsakes from his days as a star athlete at Cleveland Heights High School, as a college prankster in Wisconsin, and as a southpaw pitcher in the Milwaukee Braves' farm system. There's also his private correspondence with other rock moguls.

Belkin and I have spent many hours together, teasing out stories to spool out his life. Above all, they tell of a fabulous era in rock 'n' roll. Over the decades, Belkin created a network that continues to weave together musicians, business associates, relatives and friends while it expanded his notion of family. What's in the boxes also speaks to a work ethic, which, in his case, is a higher form of play.

Ready for tales of a bygone Cleveland, of store chases, monkeys, horses, narrow escapes, rendezvous with fame, lawsuits, settlements, failures, successes? It's high time for the reminiscences of a man who was one of the architects of the rock 'n' roll business. Read on.

Carlo Wolff
Cleveland, Ohio
September 2017

Second Warm-up Act

by Sam Belkin

I first met Mike Belkin when I was an undergraduate at the University of Miami.

Allow me to clarify. Of course, I have always known my father. The loving, caring, quick-witted, smart, and engaging man I grew up with has always been in my life. My father made the time to be in the stands at every single swim meet I competed in. He always offered helpful advice in any given scenario, provided me with countless life lessons, was quick to crack a joke, and had a story about anything you could, or even couldn't, imagine.

However, when I first met Mike Belkin, the incredibly influential powerhouse who created and shaped the Cleveland rock n' roll scene, I was in college.

My father and Annie Belkin, my mother, flew to Miami for a long weekend to escape the infamous gray and snow-laden Cleveland winter. Upon their arrival, I got a call inviting me and two of my closest friends to dinner. That evening, my friends and I arrived at the nice Japanese/Thai restaurant I had frequented before with my parents. We were college students, so it's no shock that we were a bit late. When we walked into a crowded restaurant, it was easy to spot my parents sitting at a table.

To say my father stands out in a crowd is an understatement. Dressed in his usual attire, typically comprised of a flamboyant and ostentatious (yes, both descriptors are necessary) collared shirt, tight and fashionable jeans, a nice leather belt, pristine shoes, and two unique wristwatches (each set to the same time, one on each wrist), my father stood and waved us over.

We all greeted each other, I introduced my friends, and we sat down to enjoy a nice meal. Halfway through dinner, on his second pinot grigio (his drink of choice), and with some prodding from my friends, the conversation turned towards stories about my father's time producing concerts and managing bands.

My father started by telling one of my favorite stories: the time he was invited to the Playboy Mansion in Chicago. While attempting to enjoy the experience, he also worked to maintain some measure of control over a highly inebriated Jim Morrison. But instead of the version he told to me growing up, the story—and the storyteller—suddenly transformed.

That night, my father himself became a performer, capturing my friends, and me for that matter, in his jovial story telling. I watched my father, his eyes glittering almost as brightly as the rhinestones adorning his shirt. I heard my father's strong voice, full of inflection, and truly mesmerizing. Whether it was the time away at school, my increasing age, or something else entirely, I can't say. But, in that moment, I immediately knew this person in front of me was no longer just my father. The overwhelmingly charismatic Mike Belkin had arrived.

I could write many, many pages about my father—his youth, his life, his business endeavors, his hobbies, and so much more. However, that is the purpose of what follows in this book.

Perhaps you already know of Mike Belkin and want to learn more about him or the Cleveland music scene. Maybe someone recom-

Mike and Sam Belkin in 2007.

mended this book to you or you just randomly stumbled upon it in a book review or online.

Regardless of the path that brought you here, the stories and information found in the rest of these chapters will answer many of the questions you might have about Mike Belkin, with one major exception. There is no tangible answer to, arguably, the most important question: why was Mike Belkin so wildly successful?

If you are reading this book to learn how you can replicate this success for yourself, I can save you some time. The truth of the matter is that there is no magic formula.

I know that, even though—or perhaps because—I was born after the heyday of Belkin Productions. My father had already built the production company into the an entertainment megalith. As a result, I was raised with a number of lessons from my father specifically relating to two major life goals; how to be happy and how to be successful.

The answer for the first question might seem easy and quite obvious: "Do what you love." The answer to the second question, however, is more complex. There is a saying I grew up hearing countless times come out of my father's mouth: "You don't saddle up to come in second."

In case you aren't familiar with this proverb, its origins are from horse racing. The process of training a horse, preparing it for the race, and putting on the saddle is labor- and time-intensive. The proverb's lesson is that you shouldn't go through all the trials and tribulations surrounding any endeavor if your objective is to not be the best. What goes unsaid in this interpretation is the key lesson my father imparted to me (and what he attributes his success to). You can be beaten by yourself. This is not some coy attempt to discuss political or ethical structures surrounding a career path.

The interpretation indicates that you can be the best in your field or own the most successful company. However, if you did not do the absolute best that you can, you have still come in second and wasted your efforts. The secret of Mike Belkin's success lies in the interpretation of that proverb. My father did not stop when he was successful or iconic in the Cleveland music scene. He pushed himself, and those around him, to greater levels of success because he knew he could do better. Quite simply, you never rest on your laurels. That is when you defeat yourself. My father, to this day, epitomizes this philosophy in his life.

Similar to any other business or field of study, the music industry is always changing. When my father founded Belkin Productions, there was no conception of downloading music, streaming music, posting your own music online, or any of the other possibilities enabled by the internet and digital technology. At the company's inception, there weren't even music videos. There is no question the industry—and much of life—is so different now.

But what can you gain from reading about Mike Belkin is that while technologies and even entire industries can change, history does not. Learning history, understanding history, and implementing lessons we can learn is invaluable to the contemporary world. And Mike Belkin is living history.

In many ways, he helped shape Cleveland into its current form. You will learn how Mike Belkin helped to mold Cleveland, what to expect with failure, what to expect with success, what characteristics are important to success, and what kind of person Mike Belkin is behind closed doors.

Not to mention stories about classic rock stars and industry icons. And, of course, the question I have been subjected to from the moment I could speak: what actually happens backstage at a concert?

Mike Belkin is many things and, through this book, you will come to see him fulfilling a number of different roles. But, as his son, there is something I want you to keep in mind: he is human. He is more than the sum of his successes and failures, more than the facts and figures, more than even his stories. As you read, do not forget there is a real person behind it all. The stories you will read are all real and without exaggeration. When you finish this book you will have experienced many of the stories and lessons I have been told throughout my childhood and into my adult life by my father. You will see the real Mike Belkin and the situations that surround him. If you keep his humanity in mind, you will see beyond the public figure of Mike Belkin. You will see not only my father, but the father of my siblings, Michael and Lisa, who were raised during the Belkin Productions pandemonium.

You have been given an All Access pass to go backstage and explore the history surrounding the Cleveland music scene. Just don't get distracted by the sex, drugs, and rock 'n' roll.

Sam Belkin
Cleveland, Ohio
September 2017

Chapter 1

The Old Neighborhood

This old town been home long as I remember
This town gonna be here long after I'm gone
East side, west side give but don't surrender
They been down but they still rock on...

Michael Stanley Band ~ *This Town*

It's a cold day in early 1966. Cheek glued to a black rotary phone, 31-year-old Mike Belkin is in a small back room.

The scene is Belkin's Men's Shop on West 25th Street at Clark Avenue in Cleveland, and Belkin is fielding a call from his assistant. The lanky entrepreneur is juggling information about orders, returns, credit terms, layaways—mundane but necessary details associated with running a successful clothing business.

The quarters are cramped, garment boxes are stacked high, and hangers clang on the clothing racks. At the same time, however, Belkin is making decisions that few others in the clothing business could manage. He makes notes on multiple calendars, checks and adds to long lists of names and phone numbers, calculates income and expenses, and negotiates terms with performers, venues, equipment providers and laborers.

The hours are long, impossible deadlines loom, and some days it seems impossible to make personalities and budgets fit together. But Belkin seems to have been born for a challenge like this. He's a born competitor with mettle and endurance proven during collegiate and professional sports careers. The new business that Mike Belkin is embarking on from the Belkin haberdashery looks promising.

Mike Belkin was setting sail for the new world of entertainment promotion.

Little did Belkin know that barely 10 years later, acts he presented and managed would set records and cement his place in the rock 'n' roll pantheon. From the mid-'60s to 2000, Belkin would be at the forefront of Cleveland's rock scene.

On June 25, 1977, 83,200 fans packed into the old Municipal Stadium for a Belkin production, the Pink Floyd World Series of Rock concert. In 1981, the Michael Stanley Band concert stand drew 74,404 to Blossom Music Center over four October days. Through it all, Belkin hobnobbed with the biggest acts, and was a backstage presence at mega-events like the July 1, 1978, Rolling Stones concert at the old stadium that drew 82,238 and was reportedly the first concert to gross more than $1 million.

However, that ground-breaking promoter and no-nonsense businessman has another side. He's also a sentimental guy who keeps everything. Belkin has press passes, patches and other ephemera from all these memorable events. Indeed, he has mementos from his very own beginning.

One of his most cherished keepsakes is from Mount Sinai Hospital in Cleveland, where Myron "Mike" Belkin was born on September 19, 1935. Mount Sinai gave Belkin's parents, Sam and Pola Belkin, a doll wrapped in silk cloth and little booties. The doll is a little boy, dressed in doctor's scrubs and topped with a MSH doctor's hat—for Mount Sinai Hospital. Poignantly, Belkin's doll has outlived Mount Sinai, which closed in 2000 and now is the site of a solar energy farm.

Mike Belkin in 2016.

Belkin tears up easily when speaking of his history, family and friends. He is also a "kissing person," just like his mother and Annie, his second wife. And although Belkin was particularly close to his mother, his father—called "Misha" by his wife—had his own understated way of showing affection for his younger boy, who is four-plus years younger than Sam and Pola's first-born, his brother Jules,

"He would teach me, show me, when I was working in the stores, how to do things right," Belkin says of Sam. "When you sell a suit or sport coat, you're not going to put it in a bag. You put it in a proper suit box so it's not like a rag once the customer gets it home."

His father taught him what he knew: how to operate a business and how to make money. Belkin earned his first wages in the family business early, when he was in elementary school. He dusted shoe boxes on shelves in Belkin's Cut-Rate Store on Ontario Street. Sam rewarded the boy by paying him a penny a box. Belkin realizes now, however, that more important than the pennies he earned were the lessons he learned: the tricks of the clothing trade, general business sense, and larger life lessons.

Pola Shapiro, lower left, in Russia with her friends.

One of those lessons centered on the importance of family history, and Belkin took that lesson especially to heart. Over the years, through conversations and notes, he committed to memory important family lore going back to the beginning. Belkin's mother, Pola Shapiro, a refugee from Odessa, met another refugee, Sam Belkin from Kiev. The two travelers were aboard a ship heading to New York. Their final destination would be Cleveland, likely just before the 1920s. Belkin recalls his parents speaking in Russian and Yiddish when they wanted to keep conversations private from him or his big brother Jules. Native languages were not only good for keeping secrets, though. Belkin also enjoyed a sweet taste of his heritage when his mother taught him a smattering of Russian words whenever the two of them cuddled.

From his father, Belkin's treasured keepsake is more tangible: a cigarette case dated 1905. Sam's friends in Russia signed it in Cyrillic as a present when he departed for America. It's silver, it's heavy, and

it's surely one of many special heirlooms Belkin has plans to pass on—
to Annie, of course, to his sons, Michael and Sam, and his daughter,
Lisa. For now, however, his main keepsake is this book, a long time in
the making.

Colorful Memories

"They've heard my stories and they always want to know more,"
Belkin says of his own, unusually extended family. "My son Michael
and his wife, Michele, are always asking questions and encouraging
me to write a book about my life. It has been a very colorful life, and
I've always tried things that are new and creative. That's what my life
has been. That's what I thrive on: creating and developing and want-
ing to," he searches for words, "share my life."

While he spent his infancy in Cleveland, Belkin's memories don't
begin to kick in until the family moved east of the city, to an apartment on Hampshire Road in Cleveland Heights. "I don't even think I
was in school yet," he says.

Sam Belkin and Pola Shapiro in Russia. Belkin still has the shirt Sam is wearing.

Sam and Pola Belkin at the original store.

The Coventry neighborhood, concentrated between Euclid Heights Boulevard and Mayfield Road, suited the boy well. It was a largely Jewish area of kosher meat markets, delicatessens like J. Benkovitz, bakeries and tailor shops.

"I had a wonderful childhood. Of course, there were moments I wasn't happy, but I grew up in a happy family," he says. And a distinctive one.

For one thing, he grew up with canaries, which his mom loved. He never developed a deep relationship with them, but when his parents went out of town, say for vacation, Belkin would take care of the birds in their cage in the dining room. One of his hobbies, coincidentally (don't blame the canaries) is bird watching, which he got into with Dave Jones, who was a year ahead of Belkin and a quarterback for Cleveland Heights High School.

When he was a little boy, there were few clues to his later, and defining, music business career. The Belkin household wasn't particularly musical, though Jules, who was born in 1931, took violin lessons for a while. Still, Belkin grew up exposed to many forms of music, including opera. In fact, Belkin is a big Pavarotti fan. To this day, Belkin regrets that he was unable to present Pavarotti in concert because Pavarotti's manager promoted Pavarotti's concerts himself. In Belkin's early years as a promoter, he did present Frank Sinatra, another favorite singer, not to mention one indisposed to rock 'n' roll.

Belkin was generally well-behaved, but the path to becoming a good boy takes time and involves an occasional detour. Tellingly, one of his more vivid childhood recollections is one of breaking the

Sam, Pola, Jules and Mike, seated, around 1940.

rules. It stems from his days at Coventry Elementary School and illustrates Belkin as one who likes to take the occasional risk. It was also almost a tragedy.

"I was not allowed to cross the street. But I broke the rules and I crossed the street, and a car—thank God it was a new car and had good brakes—slammed on the brakes enough to stop and just knock me over," recalls Belkin, who was five years old at the time.

Shaken but not injured, he climbed out from underneath the car and ran home to the Hampshire Road apartment—and straight into a

Mike and his father.

closet. Meanwhile, the driver, a doctor who lived nearby, asked neighborhood kids to identify the young but lucky jaywalker. The doctor soon knocked on the door of the Belkin household, shaken and angry as he told Pola about the near tragedy.

Belkin's mother quickly found her youngest son in his hiding place. Quietly but firmly she explained that she was "very disappointed." When Sam was at work, Pola could be the "sweetheart enforcer." Lesson learned: Belkin didn't cross the street that way again because he didn't want to cross his mother.

Still, nearby Coventry Road was comfortable, relatively safe and familiar, too. He remembers shopping trips with his mother for fruits and vegetables to Nutkin's grocery store, which was Jewish but not kosher, and to a kosher market for meat. At 1800 Coventry, on the southeast corner at Mayfield Road, stood the Uberstein Heights Drug Company, a Jewish drug store that he recalls fondly.

"My best memory of Uberstein's is that's where I used to go to buy ice cream. It cost five cents for a dip, seven cents for two dips," he says. Uberstein's is long gone, along with those prices. What remained over the years, however, is Belkin's sweet tooth, which would land him in trouble a little later.

Shopping and sweets were part of his early life, but so too was work. Belkin acquired the work habit when he was only seven or eight. He would ride the streetcar downtown from the Heights to help out at his parents' store on Ontario Street. On a rare Saturday off,

Mike, lower left, in a class picture from Coventry Elementary School.

Belkin would head to the Heights Theater, a movie house where he could watch a feature, preceded by a weekly serial. One of his favorite characters was the Green Hornet, who teamed with his martial artist partner, Kato, to keep city streets safe. The cost for this special Saturday entertainment: one dime.

Contrary to those quaint recollections, however, the 1,200-seat Heights Theater was also the site of mild controversy. In the '20s, the theatre broke blue laws by opening on Sundays and then in the '50s for showings of the mildly racy Louis Malle film, "Les Amants."

Taking Risks

Next door to the Heights Theater was Mitchell's Fine Chocolates, a mom-and-pop store that sold its homemade chocolate. Belkin recalls an experience there that again illustrates his appetite for candy—and risky business. He was probably a third grader at Coventry Elementary, old enough to know better "but young enough not to be put in jail."

LINER NOTES.................

Sahm Gets a Solid

Mike Belkin has always been a risk-taker, but everything he does, to this day, is from the heart. He managed, among many others, the late-lamented Doug Sahm, the great Texan singer-songwriter who headed bands spanning the Sir Douglas Quintet and the Texas Tornadoes and passed away in 1999. In the early 1970s, Belkin did Sahm a solid. The date is lost to memory but the vibe lingers on.

"I used to make sure the bands were happy and got what they needed, whether it be food or drink – whatever they needed," says Belkin. In Sahm's case, however, Belkin was almost one toke over the line.

"Doug bought some grass – he used to do a lot of marijuana –and when he was in Cleveland he ran out of marijuana, didn't have any," Belkin recalls. "So he knew somebody in Washington, and he was playing in Cleveland that night. He asked me if I would do him a favor, and I said sure. He said, 'A friend of mine has some grass for me in D.C. and I can't go there and come back in time for the concert,'" so Belkin flew there – commercial – to pick up the weed.

"I was a drug dealer," Belkin jokes. "That was out of the ordinary. He was so happy when I came home. I think he was really addicted to grass, though I don't know how you can be addicted to it. It wasn't very smart of me. I have done some stupid things in my life."

"I stole some candy from Mitchell's, and I took it home with me. My parents noticed the candy and asked if I had money to buy it— 'How did you get the candy?' " he recalls, squirming at the ancient confrontation. "I was caught, and my parents made me go back to the store and pay for the candy." That was an uncomfortable scene at home, and also uncomfortable when he made good at Mitchell's.

Overall, though, he behaved well, particularly in the bosom of his family, where he channeled his energy into an enduring taste for the theatrical. His first stage was a very familiar living room.

On weekends, Mike, his brother and his parents visited the four Belkin aunts: Sophie, Florence, Pauline and Mania, none of whom ever married. They lived together in a spacious apartment on East Boulevard. Belkin's aunts' apartment was a monument to creativi-

Mike and his father, Sam in about 1949.

Mike and Aunt Pauline at his and Annie's wedding.

ty, order, love, and art. Sophie designed hats. Pauline transformed carefully dried flowers into framed artwork. Florence was the most business-savvy, had the best sense of humor and probably was the most creative.

The youngest sister, Mania, was the only one who didn't have her own business. She was a sales person at Davis Bakery. Not important to Belkin—he adored his Aunt Mania. "She used to kid around more," he says. She was Belkin's closest contemporary in the East Boulevard household. A fifth sister never made the trip across the Atlantic.

A unique, small metal sculpture of an elephant occupied a space in the aunts' living room. When he was very young, Belkin used to sit on the elephant's back. That same elephant, minus its tusks, now sits on the ground floor of Belkin's home, a fitting testament to his aunts, Belkin's sentimental nature, and his loyalty to family memories.

An Appetite for Theater

"Mom, my dad, Jules and I would visit the aunts almost every Sunday, and they loved me a great deal as I did them," he recalls. While that East Boulevard residence reinforced a deep love of family, the setting also provided the stage for future Belkin enterprises. Encouraged by his aunts' appreciation of his thespian talents, their living room became his first stage. Those four aunts formed the first audience for Belkin—he was only five or six.

"My aunts would tell me it was time to perform," he says. "They had a small stool that would be my stage. I would walk out to the living room—the 'concert hall'—make my entrance to everybody's applause and proceed to sing songs until I was sung out, take my bows, and exit the 'stage and concert hall' thinking I was as good as Mickey Katz, 'the Yiddish Entertainer.' " (Katz was a Cleveland-born comedian and musician of no small fame, and the father of Joel Katz, better known as Joel Grey.)

Perhaps those warm family environments were a kind of vaccine—Belkin never suffered stage fright. Or maybe it was because he associates performing with a full, happy belly. "My aunts showed their affection by feeding us—wonderful dishes, in great portions," he recalls. His aunts' meals created a dilemma for Belkin, however. He couldn't possibly eat all the food he was offered, but "I didn't want to hurt my aunts' feelings, either." For young Mike Belkin, a radiator next to the kitchen table provided a handy solution. "That radiator became my 'personal receptacle' for uneaten food," he remembers. Years later, when the aunts moved from East Boulevard to Bushnell Road in University Heights, the cleanup revealed Belkin's culinary debris.

Belkin has many funny and fond memories of that stage of his life. He appeared in two shows at the Cleveland Play House—in one, he thinks he played a gingerbread man in a production of "Hansel and Gretel." And although music would come much, much later, even as a boy he'd listen to Mario Lanza 78s, transcribing the lyrics phonetically "so I could sing in a different language."

But overall, Belkin's interest in performing outside the cozy confines of the apartment waned. Nevertheless, the aunts loomed large in Belkin's overall development as did the original Cleveland Belkin, Uncle Abe, another Kiev refugee. Abe sponsored his own parents to make the same move to the United States.

Mike at his bar mitzvah with older brother Jules.

Abe and his wife, Bertha, lived on Altamont Street in Cleveland Heights. Shortly after settling in Cleveland, Abe opened the area's first extra-size men's clothing store. The year was 1920 and the store's location was Prospect Avenue near East 9th Street. A 1968 ad in *The Plain Dealer* lists 801 Prospect as a downtown landmark, "the original big & tall men's clothing store." The ad also touts Belkin's for its "We Charge It" credit card and layaway offerings, providing testament to the family's business acumen.

Details like this from nearly 100 years ago shed light on the Belkin name as being synonymous with business, innovation, and a drive to be the best. Those attributes cut across all Belkin family endeavors: clothing, sports, entertainment, sports merchandising, and community involvement. Being Belkin means being genetically entrepreneurial, innovative and predisposed to pitch in, support and help each other succeed.

A Diverse Clan

While entrepreneurship and drive were common Belkin attributes, the Belkin clan was not cut from uniform cloth. For example, Belkin's Aunt Bertha was born in the United States and was decidedly more American in culture than the other Belkins in her generation, all of whom were born in Russia. "She didn't speak Russian; it just made her a bit different," Belkin says.

"Aunt Bertha was a pleasure to be with at family affairs, though she didn't really follow the Jewish religion as much as the rest of the family." Another relative stands out in Belkin's memory as one who illustrates the latitude for individuality in the Belkin line.

Uncle Murray and Uncle Abe in June 1966 with Mike's son Michael.

This relative was Aunt Belle. While all the Belkin wives worked in business with their husbands, Belle did not. This separation was probably necessary— and a smart family decision. That's because Uncle Murray's main business was said to involve his membership in the Purple Gang, the organization which reputedly controlled Detroit's underworld in the 1920s and 1930s.

At the time, Mike Belkin couldn't possibly grasp the full scope of his uncle's "business" life. What young Belkin knew for sure, however, is that Uncle Murray was his favorite because "he was young at heart." Murray was a skilled pinochle player and also won a lot of money playing gin rummy.

In many ways, Mike Belkin is a gambler, too, as was his father, Sam. Perhaps risk-taking is in Belkin's blood. As Belkin and others would learn much later, the rock 'n' roll business, particularly in its infancy in the 1950s, would require huge gambles. But business gambles typically involve contingencies for anticipated risks—and they involve only money. Through a tragic turn involving Uncle Murray,

Belkin learned at an early age that some of the biggest gambles are personal, unknowable, and involve losses that dwarf mere dollars.

Murray and Belle were traveling by car on their way home to Detroit from Mike Belkin's bar mitzvah at Park Synagogue in Cleveland Heights. In Toledo, a cement truck violently crashed into their car. Aunt Belle was thrown from the vehicle and killed instantly, but Murray survived. Belkin learned of the tragedy from his mother while playing baseball near his Ashurst Road home in University Heights. The news shook him, but he didn't stop playing with his buddies. He still feels guilty that he wasn't more respectful or supportive. Instead, on what should be the most joyous days of a young Jewish man's life, he coped with the monumental shock the only way he knew: he played ball.

Years later, Murray remarried. His second wife was another "sweetheart" named Roz, who looked like "a young Rosalind Russell," says Belkin. Like Aunt Belle, Roz was contemporary, American, and had a good sense of humor.

Sue Rubin, Belkin's first wife, notes her own affection for Murray and Roz lasted well past her divorce from Belkin and her subsequent marriage to Stan Rubin. "Long after Stan and I married, Murray and Roz stayed with my children over a weekend. They wouldn't take any money, but he drank the whole liquor cabinet," partly stocked with premium vodka he brought from Canada.

The Essential, Entrepreneurial Belkins

Belkin's relationships with his beloved nuclear and extended family enabled him to thrive, to appreciate the value of creativity and to learn the essentials of business. Commercial aptitude for the Belkins runs deep and seems virtually a family tradition. Though the Belkin clothing business soldiered on through the 1960s, it wasn't until later that Mike Belkin would harness rock 'n' roll to truly transform the family enterprise to another level.

Before then, from a very early age he discovered a passion that he would be true to until today: sports.

Chapter 2

Career Contemplation

Taking my time
Choosin' my line
Tryin' to decide what to do

The James Gang ~ *Walk Away*

Young Mike Belkin certainly put in his hours at his parents' stores, first downtown and later at the West 25th Street and Clark Avenue location. Those were his first business schools. But time at the stores was a chore, an obligation. Away from work, Belkin spent time on two activities: school and sports. Did he like sports more than classes?

Mike, fourth from right, above, was affected by a tragic incident when he was at camp in Pennsylvania. One of the counselors, at center below, died of infantile paralysis. "They closed the camp, and all the parents had to pick up the kids," Mike says. "I had been sleeping right next to the counselor; I was quarantined for two weeks at home."

"That's a foolish question," says this distinguished clan's premier athlete. If his words seem unclear, a wry smile that accompanies his answer tells us all we need to know about his enduring love of sports.

The sport of football held little interest for Belkin, though he'd often pass around a ball in casual games of catch with friends. It was instead two other sports—basketball and baseball—that truly made Belkin's sports heart beat. And although he had many natural athletic gifts, Belkin worked hard to improve.

"I liked practice, and I always liked to be the best. So, I practiced a lot," he said.

Baseball was always his preference—Belkin is a boy of summer— but he liked basketball as well, focusing on each according to season. He became seriously interested when he was around seven years old. Always tall for his age, the leftie was a pitcher in baseball and a forward

Belkin's junior high and high school report cards portray a solid student and highlight his passion for sports.

Belkin, top left, with University of Wisconsin Pi Lambda Phi brothers.

or center in basketball. He joined teams as soon as he could, and he was good.

He worked at both sports because it was play to him, particularly once he entered high school. Belkin loved everything about games: a unique, intense hybrid of play and work. Sporting contests combine skill, competition, and live performance. A baseball or basketball game tells a story that is written by the athletes and followed by a captive audience in the grandstands. The best or luckiest team that day would get to write the ending when they won. He enjoyed writing those endings, and also enjoyed dating a cheerleader. He was a big man at Cleveland Heights High School, where he stood out in basketball and baseball.

For Belkin, though, the 1950s primarily mean baseball.

"When I was in junior high school and high school there would be summer leagues and sandlot baseball at different locations throughout the area," says Belkin. During his years at Roxboro Junior High School and later, at Heights High, he played up to three times a week, both scholastic and sandlot.

"Scholastic" of course refers to baseball played for a school, while participation in sandlot baseball was open to all players regardless of what school they attended. But make no mistake, sandlot baseball was not pick-up games—it was serious business.

"We had uniforms. We always had good coaches, whether in sandlot baseball or in academic competition. The quality of the game was virtually the same."

"For several years, we played for the same sponsor, Bissett Steel, and as a pitcher, I was active during the entire game," he says. "I really was never a good hitter, though.

"High school was high school," organized by coaches at particular schools, he says. "You could have a freshman playing in the same game as a senior, depending on the skill. Participation in sandlot baseball was also based purely on skill level, but not the school you attended, grade level or age. It depends on the league," from Class E to Class A. As might be expected, Belkin was always competing in each game, and always eager to move up a level to test and prove his ability.

Although he was naturally athletic, Belkin was so skinny his buddies called him "Bones" and "No Ass." Skinny or not, Belkin was so good, people noticed him no matter the sport. Take this quote from

Belkin in high school—number 26, center.

In high school, Belkin was a dominating player.

a Heights High School newspaper from 1951 or 1952, predicting the future of Heights' basketball team: "If I were to pick the member of the varsity who looked most promising for the future, my vote would go to a junior," said the columnist. "This power-laden scoring threat is Mike Belkin. In the games in which he has made appearances, he has exhibited his amazing variety of shots which I believe will make him one of the most valuable members of next year's squad."

That prediction was validated by a game with rival Shaker Heights High School when Mike was a senior. A game-ending buzzer beater shot he hit made him the number one scorer in the Lake Erie League. According to the *Cleveland Press*, "Belkin totaled 217 points in 12 circuit games to edge Noel Slagle of Shaker Heights, who tallied 216."

Choices, Choices

Basketball and baseball fought for Belkin's athletic attention through the '50s. Ultimately, though, you could say that baseball was responsible, at least indirectly, for paving the path to his collegiate career.

Belkin had many standout high school baseball moments, like one in 1952 when he pitched a no-hitter against East Tech. Feats like that drew attention, and he visited Kent State University at the start of 1953, his senior year at Heights High. "I cannot impress upon you too much the possibilities, both in baseball and basketball, that Kent affords you," Richard T. Paskert, the assistant coach, had written him.

In 1953, Belkin made the *Cleveland News* All-Scholastic Team. That same year, his Bissett Steel sandlot team won the Class C championship, powered by Belkin's pitching. As a result of this success, Kent State transformed its kind words into a firm offer of a baseball scholarship. That August the University of Michigan followed suit,

Belkin, second from right, front row, with the Cleveland Heights Tigers.

Belkin in his college years on the boards.

urging him to apply based on a recommendation from legendary Hall of Famer George Sisler, a U of M alumnus and a scout for the Pittsburgh Pirates.

Belkin never seriously followed up on the interest from Michigan, and he formally declined Kent State's scholarship.

But there were nonacademic suitors too, as major league baseball had Mike Belkin on its radar.

Both the Philadelphia Phillies and the Pittsburgh Pirates contacted him. Also, the legendary owner of the Brooklyn Dodgers, Branch Rickey, who broke baseball's color barrier by signing Jackie Robinson, personally scouted Belkin and watched him pitch on the sidelines.

That was as far as it went, however. The Pirates' general manager thanked him for coming and said the Pirates would be in touch. They never called; "I guess they didn't have any phones at that time," Belkin jokes.

With his professional baseball aspirations at least temporarily stalled, Belkin turned his attention to college. Following the lead of his older brother, Jules, he would become the second member of his family to attend college. But he wouldn't pursue a degree at Kent State or the University of Michigan. And while it was mostly his prowess in baseball that drew attention from pro scouts and college athletic directors, basketball—not baseball—would instead become the horse he would ride to college.

College Changes

Belkin was connected to the University of Wisconsin by the head baseball coach at Heights High in late July 1953. In a letter to the director of admissions, Belkin's coach promised that Belkin would make a good student.

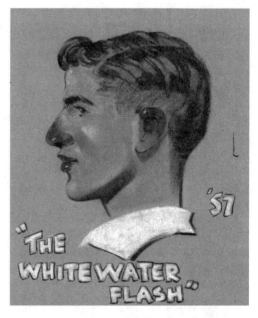

A caricature of Belkin from his Wisconsin State years.

LINER NOTES.................

All Wrapped Up

When Elvis Presley played Cleveland's Public Auditorium on June 21, 1974, Mike Belkin was a guest of Presley's California promoter. That evening, when Belkin was offered the opportunity to meet the legendary performer before the show, he eagerly accepted.

"The King," now in the late years of his reign, was camped out with his entourage in the now-defunct Swingos Hotel in downtown Cleveland, near today's growing Cleveland State University campus district. Security at Swingos was tight, but the promoter and Belkin were whisked into Presley's suite. Introductions were made but Belkin found it difficult to have a real conversation with Presley as he was being prepared to be costumed in his signature white "peacock" suit.

"I was at a loss for words," says Belkin. The reason? Presley's crew was in the midst of "wrapping him in Saran Wrap to hide how overweight he had become," says Belkin. "He put on a good show that night. But I think he was messed up; I don't know.

"When he was onstage performing, women would throw flowers on the stage. And he'd pick up a rose—and start to eat it. I always thought it was unusual to be eating flowers in the middle of the show."

Belkin, center rear, with college friends and fraternity brothers
at the University of Wisconsin.

The University of Wisconsin awarded Belkin a partial scholarship for basketball, not baseball. When Belkin made Wisconsin's varsity team as a freshman, the partial scholarship was converted to a full scholarship.

He began his freshman year at the Madison school that fall, enrolling in the pre-med program with an eye toward becoming a dentist. His pre-med career stalled after his freshman year, however.

At the start of his sophomore year, Belkin was expelled for violating school rules. The incident involved Belkin and three classmates persuading a town resident to pose for semi-nude pictures. Unbeknownst to Belkin and his three classmates, the girl was dating a Madison cop, which likely added to the attention the matter received.

According to a wire story from December 8, 1954, "Wisconsin University has expelled four students involved in a 'Hollywood talent scout' incident in which a girl posed" for topless photographs. The story did not identify the students, but noted that five others were placed on disciplinary probation in connection with the incident.

Belkin in high school.

Belkin had persuaded the girl that he had Hollywood connections and that his father was a producer. The university called Belkin's father and Sam Belkin immediately flew north to explain that he was indeed not a producer—and to collect his wayward son. The two packed up the 20-year-old's belongings and made a quiet trip home to Cleveland to decide the next phase of his life

"I wasn't sure what was going to happen," says Belkin, recalling his apprehension about his father. "There was no confrontation. He asked me what's going on, what happened." Belkin told him the truth, they flew back together, "it passed." Sam Belkin was supportive, mostly, Mike suspects, because of his complete admission as well as the joint realization that the matter might have turned out far more seriously. Sam took action in the way he knew best—by immersing his son's attentions back in the family business, where he and other family members could guide him.

So Belkin spent the summer of 1955 working at his family's clothing outlets in Cleveland, Painesville and Ashtabula. At the same time, he continued pursuing his academic career.

Within the year, Belkin would return to the Badger State. He enrolled at Wisconsin State College-Whitewater, located in a college town midway between Madison and Milwaukee. He gave up pre-med—"I hated physics, but it was a requirement"—but maintained his connections

Enjoying a day off in Corpus Christi.

At the store in Painesville.

to sports. He played basketball, and also pitched for Whitewater State Teachers College. Whitewater athletics, he says, were less challenging than Madison had been.

Whitewater State at that time wasn't an NCAA school, but its location, only an hour's drive north of Milwaukee, provided an opportunity that Belkin discovered—and seized.

"When the Milwaukee Braves finished their spring training and came up to Milwaukee for the regular season, I would drive down. I'd warm up on the sidelines with pitching coaches watching me," Belkin says. The sound of a Belkin fastball hitting the mitt was also the sound of the door to professional baseball opening, if just a crack.

Going Pro

As a result of the attention and exhibition, the Milwaukee Braves signed him as a semi-pro in late August, 1955. He pitched for the Class AA Texas League Beaumont Exporters in 1955 and the Class B Big State League Corpus Christi Clippers in 1956. Upon completion of his junior year at Whitewater State, he took a big step by committing to professional baseball for two years.

But he couldn't make the commitment on his own. Because he was not yet 21 years old, his parents had to sign for him.

Belkin sets the scene: "We were in the back of the store, there was a table, and a scout from the Milwaukee Braves came in with the contract," Belkin recalls. While Sam and Pola had the legal authority to sign the contract, Mike Belkin had the knowledge of the business of baseball, so he negotiated the terms of the deal, he says.

He signed for $4,000 plus $200 a month during the season.

One of the caveats of the contract "was that I would be able to finish my semesters at college and then go down to play professional baseball." So he was able to complete his college studies each year, a condition that was important to his parents.

The $4,000 bonus—for context, that represented about $35,000 in 2017 dollars—was the maximum amount that professional baseball allowed at the time; anything more and you'd "be considered a bonus baby," depriving an experienced major leaguer of a roster spot, Belkin says.

Major League Baseball only allowed two bonus babies and the Braves already had their two that year; that's why the $4,000 was the ceiling for Belkin.

Besides, he says, "I wasn't putting in a whole year," deferring to the education component his parents wanted.

At Corpus Christi, Belkin was an effective hitter, posting a .375 batting average. "I always say those were the best years of my life," Belkin says of his Texas seasons. He was enjoying life, and "because I was playing, I wasn't really working. I was getting paid $200 a month," providing him with plenty of money for food and hotel rooms, not to mention spending cash.

"No obligations, and I was dating a lot," Belkin recalled. "Women are always going after baseball players."

The manager his first year was an old-timer by the name of Mickey Livingston. "One day he said to me"—Belkin assumes a southern drawl—"he said, 'Mike, you're going to fuck your way out of baseball.'"

Into the 1980s, Mike Belkin often played in Michael Stanley's pickup ball games.

Stan Grossman, from left, Sandy Weisman and Mike Belkin, all friends since fourth grade.

What could I say?"

Was he right? "Probably," Belkin cracks up.

There was one time in Beaumont that he dated Texas twins. No pictures survive. "It's not like I was in bars, hustling," Belkin says. These girls used to come to the games. The twins were friendly and sexy and he had separate relationships with them.

In his own understated style, Belkin says, "Those were fun times."

Shifting Gears

All good things must come to an end, however. In the summer of 1956, Belkin quit pro baseball for a number of reasons. One of his sentiments was "I wasn't playing enough," he says. "I felt I didn't have the chance to show my goods enough."

Perhaps the seeds of Belkin's discontent were sown as a result of a stipulation in his original deal that allowed him to skip spring training in order to attend college. While he appreciated the arrangement, looking back he sees that he was never properly prepared—"I never really had any regular spring training experience," he says.

Race consciousness also played a part. As a Jew, Belkin was sensitive to segregation. On virtually every team, he was the only Jew, and while he never felt any prejudice directed at him, he was uncomfortable with a black-and-white world. "Living at that time and being from the North and seeing first-hand how blacks were treated in a totally different way than white people" disturbed Belkin. "When we would go into other cities to play a game, black players and the clubhouse manager were not allowed to stay in the same hotels and had to be dropped off in black neighborhoods. It made me feel like 'Whitey.'"

He came to view himself as a man of privilege, enjoying time playing a sport. "I wasn't thinking of money because I knew I had this job at home with my dad. It wasn't, like, make it or you don't make it."

"Baseball was the sole livelihood for many players. I'm looking at all these guys who came up from nothing; this had to be their life," he explains.

As for writing off sports as a profession, Belkin admits he was into baseball for the fame. "I do regret that I wasn't as good as I thought I was," he says. "I was doing it for me, really, to be Mike Belkin, a big game winner." On a final reflection, Belkin says that "maybe I saw the handwriting on the wall. For me, I knew once I was playing that I wasn't as good as I thought I was. I decided it was a great 2 ½ years, I'm going to go back to college."

So in mid-1956, Mike Belkin packed his Texas bags and came home to Cleveland to play Class A sandlot baseball for Al Naiman Wreckers. He also came home questioning his career and life path.

He seemed to find several answers at his next move when he enrolled as a business major at Western Reserve University. The dean of men, who went by Dean Kramer, was "very instrumental in helping me through my college days at Western Reserve," Belkin says. And as Belkin began to focus on business at Western Reserve, he continued helping his parents with their enterprises.

On the personal side, on that same campus, a mutual acquaintance introduced him to Sue Harrison. He married Sue on December 22, 1957, at Park Synagogue and just over a month later, he graduated from Western Reserve, ready to begin the next phase of his life.

If music was not yet a main focus, it had begun to play in the background of Belkin's life.

"To me, music was mostly something to dance to at high school dances," he says, noting that in high school he did come to appreciate the allure of the music business—sort of.

A man named Don Koplow, who was in the same class as Belkin, recorded a minor hit in 1952 called "Oh Happy Day" under the name of Don Howard. Belkin recalls that in a Heights basketball team visit to Warren, Ohio, girls from that city clamored for Howard, and Heights cheerleaders pointed to Belkin—as if he were Howard. Someone else ultimately stood in for Howard, signing autographs for his Warren fans.

Belkin saw the power of music—and he was hooked.

Chapter 3

Music's Siren Song

I caught your waves last night
It sent my mind a-wonderin'.

Sir Douglas Quintet ~ *Mendocino*

Tracing Mike Belkin's personal path that would eventually lead to his musical and promotional enterprise requires grounding in his business schooling. It wasn't just the coursework at Western Reserve University in the mid-1950s that prepared him for his trailblazing business career. It was also growing up in his parents' clothing business and learning from role models he met through them—and then creatively consolidating and applying all that he learned.

Belkin recalls the neighborhood around the Ontario store as quite colorful. For all we know, fashion impressions he absorbed there would influence the rock 'n' roll business he got involved in much later.

"Our store was next to a store that was rented by gypsies who would tell fortunes, and my dad actually was a friend of the king of the gypsies," he says. "Gypsies had and still do have this reputation of being dishonest."

The term "gypsy" is slang for the Romani people, and has many popular associations, most of them negative: they're drifters, superstitious, cunning, and above all, mysterious and prone to deception, if not outright theft.

In fact, a poll of the social standing of 58 ethnic groups in a 1992 issue of *The New York Times* reported that gypsies were at the very bottom. However, Belkin and his family saw the so-called gypsies differently. "They would never steal from my dad or the store. In fact, they didn't wear the clothes my dad would sell. They would dress much nicer. They dressed in high style."

In addition to continuing to develop his keen appreciation for both alternative styles and diverse cultures, Belkin learned how to squeeze a dollar.

For example, his father would buy inventory from a troubled store and run a going-out-of-business sale. Belkin's dad taught him that's "the best sale you can possibly have. It attracts people more than any other sale," Belkin says. Sam was a liquidator when he could buy at a good price. In one large deal, Sam Belkin liquidated the inventory in a three-level department store near Cleveland when his son was in college at the University of Wisconsin.

"What he would do is buy all the merchandise in the store and then he would go out and buy additional merchandise, price it high and then slash the price," says Belkin. Signs all over the store would trumpet those bargains; it was not the only way the younger Belkin learned about the mix of price and promotion from his dad.

Lessons in Salesmanship

Belkin also had a good teacher in Henry Lifshitz, a Cleveland man he said originally owned Uncle Bill's stores, an early local discount chain. Lifshitz personally introduced young Belkin to New York's fabled garment district, taking him on a trip to show Belkin the ropes of the clothing business. Lifshitz did this out of the goodness of his heart, Belkin says.

"He was a good friend of my dad's. A lot of people can tell you how to sell.

In front of the meat counter at the Painesville store.

"Harry was special because he taught me how to buy," says Belkin.

On his first buying trip to New York for the discount stores, they went to the garment center, around 34th Street and Broadway, getting special access into showrooms as they went from store to store.

"I loved it," says Belkin, a perpetual kid in a candy store. "I liked the fact that I was there and seeing the merchandise, being able to negotiate and figure out how much to buy." He would look for closeouts that would last at least a season, "depending on the price I could negotiate."

Back at home, he also learned the value of vigilance as related to security.

One incident Belkin recalls vividly involved a couple that ran out of a store his father was liquidating on Pearl Road. Sam Belkin noticed that suits on hangers were missing from a spot where a woman had just been—and that the man and the woman left the store rather hurriedly. "My dad yelled out, 'she stole a suit,' " collared the woman and made her stay in the store, according to Belkin.

"I and a friend, Marvin Whay, ran out after the man and caught him and brought him back into the store. How stupid can you get?" says Belkin, who was studying business at Western Reserve University at the time. "My dad took the guy—he wasn't a small guy—pushed him and held him to the counter. Then my dad pretended to have a gun in his back pocket, telling me to lock the door and call the police."

As for the man's companion, not only did she steal one suit, she had two others on hangers underneath her dress. Both people were charged with theft.

Besides his savvy and boldness in addressing thefts, his father also knew and employed some classic merchandising approaches. Sam would take old inventory, mark it up—and then mark it down. The idea was to make the customer "feel like they're getting a real good buy," Belkin says, adding his father also would bring merchandise he'd bought into the store and initially put a higher price tag on it. "Say he bought it for $5, he would mark it up to $15, $20, then mark it down to $10." Such a deal.

"Because of the type of store it was, whatever you bought to sell you'd plan on going down on price. You could bargain there, which I really liked once I knew what the item actually cost," says Belkin, who enjoys the back-and-forth. First, however, he had to learn the fine art of the haggle.

One day, at the Ontario store, he told a customer the marked cost of a pair of pants and the customer said it was too much. "I didn't know our actual cost and what I could sell it for and still make a profit, so he walked out of the store without purchasing anything."

Afterwards, Belkin's dad approached him and said, "Myron, I want to tell you a story.

"Imagine a customer walked out of the store and told me he'd be back later to buy something. And then he moved out of town, or crossed the street and got hit by a car or something," his dad said. Beyond the blunt tone of the story, the message Belkin took from the allegory was, "You get a customer in the store, you sell him when he's in the store. You may never have another chance."

From then on, Belkin always made sure to know what his father wanted to charge so if he had to, he could bargain and nail down a sale. And he employed that practice of knowing as much as possible and then applying the information urgently to other facets of his business.

In 1949, Sam and Pola Belkin needed to apply what they knew and then respond intelligently and with urgency when the couple suffered a devastating business setback. The Belkin clothing business was effectively displaced after Cleveland's storied Central Market burned down. The couple was forced to shutter the original Belkin's Cut Rate Store on Ontario Street downtown. But in true Belkin form, rather than just give up, they adapted to the situation and opened its successor, Belkin's Men's Shop, at Clark Avenue and West 25th Street.

Even though their business moved a relatively short distance west, Sam and Pola Belkin's business changed quite a bit.

While the Ontario Street location catered largely to Russian and central European immigrants, the location at West 25th catered to "a different clientele," largely Puerto Ricans and Italians, according to Belkin. It also was more upscale and the store needed more manpower.

Belkin worked in the store on Saturdays starting when he was very young—and when he was older, during vacations from school. He was not happy about that.

"I remember that the kids were playing basketball on Saturdays at elementary school and I couldn't play," he says. "I had to go and work for my parents. However, I was making some big bucks." Among other emoluments, he got a penny a box to dust a shoebox and a nickel to assemble a suit box. "I was a specialist," he jokes. "I think that was in lieu of a weekly allowance."

Mike Belkin married Sue Harrison on December 22, 1957, at Park Synagogue.

The work could be hazardous; Belkin is fortunate he still has fingertips, "because to put price tags on apparel at that time you needed two pins, and each price tag was perforated, so you had to put the price tag in straight and then crimp the pins so the tag would stay on the garment."

Sam Belkin worked six days a week, so Sundays were important to him because he could sleep in. "Sunday morning we had to be quiet; it was a small apartment," says Belkin of the family's Hampshire Road domicile.

During that era, the message for the Belkin boys was very clear: "Don't bother dad."

The Belkin Expansion

In the late '50s, Belkin's parents extended their apparel enterprise to Painesville and Ashtabula, so Belkin's commitment to the family business deepened as well. And since his graduation from Western Reserve on January 31, 1958, he was free to work. Had to work and make it work, in fact, with his own new family in the making.

First came a Painesville expansion when the Belkins leased space for their men's clothing operation in a building that otherwise was occupied, unlikely enough, by a meat packing operation. The move was made possible by the graduation of Jules and Mike. This was a big move, and a big commitment; at that time, Belkin and his bride Sue were living in an apartment on Shaker Boulevard; he made the 75-minute trip to Painesville far too often.

Besides the expansion of store locations to a city more than an hour away, the Belkins at the same time expanded their clothing offerings. Long known for selling men's clothing, in Painesville the Belkins now offered womens' and girls' apparel, an extension made possible by Belkin's experience with Henry Lifshitz in New York City.

"I would go to a manufacturer in New York, we would talk and develop a relationship, so if I needed a favor … it's all personal relationships," Belkin says. "Why am I doing business with you if we don't have a relationship?" It was and is a constant with Mike Belkin: he's built virtually everything on business relationships, many of which developed into strong friendships that endure.

In New York, his buying approach was twofold; one "what was happening today, especially for women." Secondly, he'd pay attention to "last season's closeouts, and that was the advent of imports, that's when they started." In Painesville, he began selling "clothes made in China. They were terrible, but they were cheap."

"Make that inexpensive. Inexpensive sounds more classy."

Painesville merchandise was indeed a cut below, Belkin admits. He would sell a men's suit there for $29.99, throwing in an extra pair of pants for $9.99. What were these made of? "Paper," he wisecracks. Actually, that suit was made of rayon acetate—"God help you if you sat down and got up"—and didn't hold its crease. He didn't wear these himself, he says, nor would he sell those in the men's store; the wool suits the family sold in Cleveland were better quality—and pricier, too.

At West 25th Street, the Belkins also sold communion suits, and "we would rent out tuxedos for weddings and special events; that was a good business." Word-of-mouth carried the Belkin name and the results were referrals and a lot of repeat business. "We had a good reputation; people knew Belkin's Men's Shop." They also knew Belkin through his Uncle Abe, whose Belkin's Men's Store on Prospect Avenue was the first men's store in the city that sold extra-size apparel. In fact, both Belkin's parents' store and his uncle's store specialized in clothes for big men.

In addition to honing his buying and selling expertise in clothing, Belkin ventured into promotion. In an early example of his promotional flair, Belkin brought in a new business partner: a spider monkey. He bought the monkey to display at the Seaway Discount Store in Painesville, where the family ran its first non-Cleveland operation. "It wasn't a real big monkey," Belkin recalls. "I wanted to have the children come in and see the monkey, so I added a cage, and on top of it, we had a table and I hand-built more shelves for merchandise.

"I put the monkey in a cage and put it on the upper shelf and people would come, kids would see it, and at night, we would take it home to the Cleveland apartment and we'd take it out the next day."

It's probably appropriate at this time to put the monkey, named Paco, into the "it seemed like a good idea at the time" category.

Belkin says, "The next day the monkey took its food and water and spilled it all over everything in the store—and on the merchandise."

Sue adds that "Mike kept him at the store, but that was a problem because he'd throw things out of the cage." Horrified by the damage and aggravated by the distraction, Belkin made the decision: the monkey had to go. Paco, however, took the rejection hard. The hammer finally came down when Paco fancied himself as an automobile enthusiast.

"We're driving back home to the apartment, I had to stop and get something from the drugstore and the monkey's sitting in Sue's lap," Belkin says. "I came out of the drugstore and I see Sue sitting in the

Mike and Sue's son, Michael, was born on April 19, 1960.

passenger seat and she's crying, and I see the monkey holding the steering wheel, like it was driving. When he sees me coming, he lets go of the steering wheel, jumps into her lap."

Belkin asked Sue why she was crying. "The minute you left he bit me and jumped behind the steering wheel," she told him.

While Belkin sounds like he could have killed the monkey, Sue is less harsh and even forgiving. "The monkey was just wonderful," she says. While the monkey was in the driver's seat, Sue says that Paco "mimicked everything; touched the key, adjusted the mirror," pretending he was driving. But because of the bite, Mike took her to the hospital, where Sue endured a painful but necessary tetanus shot.

Sealing Paco's fate was what happened later that night when they finally made it to their apartment. "That night, at home, by mistake he gets out of his cage and he was fucking crazy, running all around hanging by the drapes, he shits while he's hanging from the drapes," Belkin continues.

"That was it. I called up the guy, said I can't have this monkey anymore, he doesn't listen, he's crazy and I don't want a death on my hands. The guy bought the monkey back."

While the monkey incident may have been a highlight of Belkin's tenure at the Painesville store, it was his relationship with a prominent Ashtabula businessman that would prove to have a far more positive, less traumatic, and more lasting effect on his business.

Because there were no highways then, each leg of the trip from home to Painesville took Belkin an hour and 15 minutes—in good weather. He worked six days a week from 9 a.m. to 9 p.m. and Sundays from 9 to 6. "I drove that fucking road seven days a week," says Belkin, who reached Euclid Avenue from Shaker Boulevard and East 108th Street, where he and Sue lived in an apartment across from St. Luke's Hospital.

As if that expansion eastward in Ohio wasn't enough, the Belkins continued to explore new geographies and new opportunities. When Mike and Sam Belkin scouted out a possible Ashtabula Belkin's men's clothing outlet for expansion, the two eventually met LeRoy V. Anderson in Anderson's store. "LeRoy and my dad got along famously," Belkin says. Anderson sold major appliances, hardware and housewares in his prosperous store.

An agreement was forged, and the Belkins partnered to begin joint operations in LeRoy Anderson's store.

Mike would spend time both in the Belkins' Painesville store and in Anderson's Department Store in Ashtabula, "a nicer space" than the one in Painesville, he remembers. Meanwhile, the Belkins also maintained the Cleveland store on West 25th Street; Jules and Sam ran that while Mike was in charge of the discount stores.

Eventually, Sam had a heart attack and was semiretired when he died in 1966, and Jules essentially took over the West Side store. Although their father was gone, the memory of Sam and the lessons he taught remained. It was time for Jules and Mike to be completely in charge of the family's future. And a portent of what direction that future would take was at that store in Ashtabula.

The music office at Anderson's was in the main part of the store. Equipped with a telephone, it served both as customer service area— and indirectly, as a prototype for a Belkin Productions office that would follow a bit later.

Socks Forever

The Belkin elders and Anderson and his wife—"he was a big guy, she was a peanut"—got along famously, even vacationing together in Puerto Rico. And as usual, when Mike Belkin was involved with a businessman he liked and respected, he learned and grew. That was the case with LeRoy Anderson.

"I learned from him that the best salesmen have the best personalities," says Belkin. "He had a very good personality and was an excellent sales person. That's just who he was." Major manufacturers would have sales contests based on the quantity of retail sales, giving away vacations to successful retailers like Anderson. Belkin took note of the concept of the promotion as well as Anderson's success; when he wasn't making his own sales, Belkin would watch Anderson in action.

But generally, Belkin was too busy, particularly with socks.

"I had a weakness for socks, and for Ashtabula I had purchased thousands of socks, probably 2,000 socks unpaired, which came in big cardboard cartons. So when they came in, they had to be matched up. I bought them for 30 cents a pair, but you had to pair them up.

"I wanted to be the king of socks, and I succeeded," says Belkin. "I'm still buying and selling socks, the difference being that the socks I was selling back then I was selling for 39 cents a pair. The socks I'm selling today are all licensed sports socks that I'm selling for $7.50 wholesale to supermarket chains and drug chains."

One of his best socks items is the Ohio State University variety. Recently, he bought 1,400 pair of OSU socks. "Right now before I ordered them, I had zero socks," he says. Did you get a good deal? "No, as a matter of fact he raised the price on me.

"When you're a buyer, it's a challenge that you have the knowledge or the taste that will satisfy a customer so that they will purchase it. So you have to have some of that feel for the customer out there. It ties in for me with the music business." You have to stay current with trends and "be able to purchase at the right price so it will sell to the consumer."

The Business Mentality

"Being a business person is getting a feel for what the traffic will bear," he says. "Whatever I've done, my brain works the same way for all the businesses—the clothing business, the concert business, the sports business."

Sports merchandising became Belkin's focus late in his life, and to Belkin, there's always been a connection between sports and music. That connection would be made explicit in the World Series of Rock he later launched in 1974.

Mike, standing, and Jules, left, in a 1964 meeting.

Those mega-shows, which ended in 1980, may have been the culmination of a business Belkin entered nearly 20 years earlier. But they might not have taken flight with the same trajectory had Belkin not become associated with Anderson's, particularly with the store's sideline: promoting shows at the Swallows, a swank eatery in downtown Ashtabula.

When it comes to music promotion, Belkin acknowledges that he took his cues primarily from Anderson. Another influence would be John Kenley, an entrepreneur said to have revolutionized summer stock theater.

"Being in the store with LeRoy and knowing what was going on at the Swallows, I decided I was going to look at a Cleveland paper and see what was happening concert-wise in Cleveland," he says. "What I saw was that the Beach Boys had played, Peter Paul & Mary had played, but those shows were few and far between.

LINER NOTES.................

Another Saturday Night...

Belkin Productions had partners on all seven dates of a 1974 Cat Stevens tour except for one at Public Hall in Cleveland that April 23. The tour ran from April 22 to July 10. Mike Belkin toed a very fine, potentially dangerous line—make that lines—at one of those dates.

Stevens' manager and attorney were friends, "which is how we got the tour," Belkin says.

Stevens was one of the first rock stars to bring his own chef and cook on tour, and he used to make dinner before the show. "He was very quiet," says Belkin. "It was nice. It was easy."

Belkin, who was single at the time, brought a date to one of the gigs, either in Chicago or Detroit, and he behaved himself. "The keyboard player for Cat Stevens invited us to his hotel room and he brings out the coke and lines it up and said, come on, let's do it," he recalls. "She did it," the keyboard player said of Belkin's date.

"He said to me, come on, do it. I didn't snort it—I faked it. He didn't know, but she did. And she did whatever was left. There was a lot left."

"Another company was promoting in Cleveland at that time," he said, "but most of what it did was classical. Victor Borge was a booking, the Ukrainian Dance Company was a booking. "

And during the summer—and only during the summer—the competition was Musicarnival, the outdoor tent John L. Price ran at 4401 Warrensville Center Road in Warrensville Heights from 1954 to 1975.

So in the mid-'60s, the Belkins saw an opening in local concert promotion, especially when it came to rock 'n' roll and more contemporary music. There was a vacuum, Belkin realized. And there were business lessons to learn from men like Anderson and Kenley, a business visionary whose Kenley Players was changing the entertainment landscape. Kenley was credited with pioneering the notion of putting veteran Hollywood performers and television personalities into summer stock productions.

Belkin knew Kenley personally but only in passing. The two shared a cab ride from LaGuardia into Manhattan to a hotel.

"Kenley was not only making waves," says Belkin, "he was very successful at what he was doing." Ironically, if the Belkins had been more successful in raising enough money, they might have gone into Kenley's type of show business, Jules told the music trade magazine *Pollstar* in 1990.

"Actually, there was a time before that when we almost became summer stock producers," Jules said.

"Kenley Players shows were expensive productions and we didn't have that kind of money," Belkin recalls. So he hired an attorney to draw up an agreement designed to help raise money to produce musicals at the Hanna Theatre. That's the near miss his brother referred to.

In an effort to emulate Kenley's success in Warren, the brothers tried to raise $100,000 in partnership with a group of people in Cleveland with money and similar interests. It didn't work.

"We set a goal of $100,000 and if we couldn't raise it, then we would just forget it," Jules told *Pollstar*. "I think we raised about $85,000 and had a tough time with the last $15,000, so we dropped it. That was our first attempt at show business."

Their second attempt, which initially involved Ashtabula businessman Anderson, was more successful. It built upon what Anderson started, before eventually rising to a new level.

Anderson's approach to music promotion was centered mostly on driving traffic into the store. "So he started booking and promoting big bands, primarily in a place called the Swallows, a restaurant-club in downtown Ashtabula. He would promote the big bands and sell tickets at a very reasonable price," says Belkin, referring to the "Anderson's Department Store Presents" series.

At the Swallows, Anderson presented Louis Armstrong, Lionel Hampton and Duke Ellington, among other big bands, Belkin says, noting he himself was never interested in presenting such groups. He was interested in promoting more contemporary kinds of shows in Cleveland.

Cleveland Beckons

Anderson's successful musical promotion started wheels turning in Belkin's head. "Maybe we could be doing something in Cleveland," he told Anderson. So they became partners in early Cleveland shows, though not in Ashtabula. Jules was part of the partnership too.

"Anderson was doing small shows in a small venue in a small city, but he was supplying 50 percent of the investment," with the brothers splitting the other 50 percent; so initially, Anderson was the main moneyman. "Jules and I had no experience in promoting concerts; we didn't even know who we were going to present for the first concert." Anderson, other than lending his name and backing, had nothing to do with that booking.

Anderson was a good promoter both in his store and in the Swallows concerts, some of which did well, others not so well. He'd advertise "Anderson's Department Store Presents" shows on local radio, along with his primary business, selling tickets both at his store and at the Swallows.

Belkin summarizes the promoter's challenge: "Ultimately you have to sell tickets, you have to know who you can partner with and trust to help you sell tickets, and where your potential customers are," says Belkin.

"And then it sounds so simple, but it's not. It takes a lot of balls, too. When you're putting out your cash, it's not so easy. There's pressure. Am I advertising in the right place? Am I spending money in the right place?"

Actually, Belkin says, after he saw how little pop activity was going on in Cleveland and how effectively Anderson was booking into the Swallows, "I asked LeRoy if he wanted to be a partner in producing concerts in Cleveland. That's when Belkin & Anderson was born, and Leroy asked if I'd do the booking."

Anderson had restricted his bookings to presenting big bands in Ashtabula, but big bands were on their way out. Belkin had different ideas; he wanted to expand into Cleveland with something fresh.

He told Anderson and his brother the three should present contemporary music in the much larger city, but neither had a favorite artist he wanted to present. Belkin, however, had just the right group in mind. Or so he hoped.

"I came up with the Four Freshmen because I liked their music," he says.

So the first-time music producer called the agency for the Four Freshmen. The parties agreed on the fee ($1,750) and a date (February 5, 1966). "And then the agent asked me who was the opening act and I said, 'I don't think I understand.

"What's an opening act?' "

The agent explained that Belkin needed "someone to be first, before the headliner, and I said, 'who do you have?' " He recommended the New Christy Minstrels, a group he also represented. Belkin didn't know who they were; booking an unknown group and incurring an additional, unexpected cost upped the ante for the production. But Belkin signed on anyway, and music promotion officially began for the Belkins.

Belkin & Anderson was the alliance that presented that Four Freshmen-New Christy Minstrels show. Mike Belkin handled the booking, Jules did the advertising and Anderson was very much a silent partner. In a way, the show was a success; it came off without a hitch, and the fans were pleased by the group and the new opportunities. Financial success for Belkin & Anderson? That's a different matter.

Ticket prices ranged from $3 to $6.50. At first, the brothers thought they had cleared $60 in profit. In fact, whether they profited and what the final figure was are matters of dispute. In a video interview former Rock and Roll Hall of Fame and Museum executive James Henke did for *Pollstar*, Jules said a recent review of Belkin Productions' earliest contracts shows that first show actually lost about $35. "I always thought it was $67," Mike Belkin wryly says of the missing profits. "I always wondered where that $10 went."

That first concert might not have been profitable, but it was invaluable. They learned they must pay attention to the basics: staging, advertising, marketing, insurance and staffing, Jules told *Pollstar*. He called it "a learning experience, very quickly under fire," noting he didn't even attend because he started his vacation that very night.

Belkin Productions quickly evolved into a Cleveland operation run out of the family's men's store on West 25th Street. That was the location of Belkin Productions' first real office, with a telephone number separate from the store's operation. The office, in the back near the air-conditioning unit, was "very small," probably 10 feet by 6 feet.

The Freshmen-Minstrels date convinced the Belkins they were on the right track. At least until the next show.

Make that "No Show."

Chapter 4

Belkin Productions Stakes its Claim

Now first it wasn't easy
Changin' Rock and Roll and minds...

Wild Cherry ~ *Play That Funky Music (White Boy)*

The success of the Four Freshmen-New Christy Minstrels show in February 1966 told Mike and Jules Belkin that they were on to something new and potentially very lucrative. Agents began to recognize them as Cleveland-area powers, approaching Mike with acts that attested to the growing clout of rock 'n' roll. The brothers were ready to present, even when the acts weren't.

Cleveland had been musically active for some time, as evidenced by some signature performances and events. Presented by legendary DJ Alan Freed, the Moondog Coronation Ball in the old Cleveland

Arena on March 21, 1952, is widely cited as the first rock 'n' roll concert. Elvis Presley had celebrated his 20th birthday and the release of his first single, "Heartbreak Hotel," just a month before he played the Circle Theater on February 26, 1955; he returned to play a show at Brooklyn High School that October 20. Leo's Casino became a Euclid Avenue music magnet starting in 1962, the same year Jane Scott launched her teen beat column in the *Plain Dealer*. The Rolling Stones performed at Public Hall on November 3, 1964, and the Beatles played Public Hall on September 15, 1964, and two years later at Cleveland Stadium on August 14. Nevertheless, even with this concert and venue track record, rock 'n' roll was not yet the cultural mainstay that the Belkins would help make it. But it certainly seemed promising to be active in promoting rock 'n' roll music in Cleveland and the Midwest.

Still, the entertainment landscape in mid-'60s Cleveland was largely conservative. Giacomo Bernardi, manager of the Cleveland Opera Association, who booked the likes of the Bolshoi Ballet, ruled the classical field. According to a *Plain Dealer* article following his death in 1966, Bernardi "played a large part in bringing Cleveland cultural events of almost all types." In addition, Warren's John Kenley presented theater by way of his Kenley Players. And there was Musicarnival, an outdoor tent theater in the round in Warrensville Heights.

Breaking the Mold

The Belkins weren't that interested in either classical presentations or Broadway variants, however—at least not yet. Instead, they were beginning to sniff out rock 'n' roll opportunities.

The second Belkin & Anderson booking was the Mamas and the Papas. The folk-rock group, composed of John Phillips, Denny Doherty, Cass Elliot and Michelle Phillips, had been cruising the radio airwaves with such hits as "California Dreamin' " and "Monday, Monday." Unfortunately, without even performing, the Mamas and the Papas caused the neophyte Belkin & Anderson production company to reconsider its new endeavor.

With advice from LeRoy Anderson, this is the first production by the young Belkin promoters. This ad is from the Sunday, January 23, 1966 Plain Dealer.

In 1966, the Mamas and the Papas were set for Public Hall. The first booking fell through because of drug use in the band, though the ostensible reason given to the public was "that one of them was ill," says Belkin. Once was bad enough, but what followed shook the fledgling promotion firm to its core.

"Then we had a remake with a new date and they gave us the same bullshit. Meanwhile, we had spent money on advertising, ticket printing, ticket selling—and ticket refunds." At least Belkin & Ander-

LINER NOTES.................

A Man of His Word

Tim LaRose, a wholesale beverage executive whose accounts include Budweiser beer and Monster energy drinks, was a major Belkin Productions partner from near the beginning. He tells this story from when he was a sophomore at Archbishop Hoban in Akron, hearing KYW's Jerry G. announce that Jimi Hendrix was coming to Cleveland's Music Hall.

"Three buddies and I drive up to Cleveland Hopkins Airport and hide the car and we're paranoid as shit, we're cutting school, and we take the train downtown to Public Square. We get to KYW, say we need tickets for the Jimi Hendrix show. So they say, what you got to do is go over to Belkin Brothers Clothing Store.

"We're these four ragtag kids and this big, tall guy, this giant man comes walking up, hovering over us, looks down at us and says, what are you kids doing in here? We're kind of shaking in our boots because we're still thinking we're going to get picked up for cutting school.

"The guy looks at us: why aren't you in school? Because we have to see this. He says, you got your money? Yes, sir. He comes walking back, points at me and says, write your name and address on here. Get your ass back to school, you understand? Yes sir, yes sir. If you get your ass back to school, I'll send you the tickets."

Maybe six weeks pass. "Then all of a sudden one day there's an envelope and four tickets in there, second row, dead center."

That big tall guy was Mike Belkin. "He did a wonderful thing."

son got partial compensation for the cancellations from the band's management. The refund to Belkin & Anderson was probably driven less by business propriety and more by fear that the real reason for the cancellations—drug abuse—might leak to the general public.

The whole tour was canceled, and the Belkins had to refund the tickets and absorb the promotional costs, not to mention the costs of renting Public Auditorium. The Mamas and the Papas was such a fiasco, Jules Belkin told *Pollstar*, that the brothers considered pulling out of their fledgling business.

Fortunately, a successful jazz show convinced them to stay the course.

Despite that rocky start, the Belkins already had a reputation. So when George Wein was looking to book a Cleveland date for a northern Ohio version of a jazz festival he already had slotted for Cincinnati, a promotions man at WJW-AM suggested the Belkin brothers.

The WJW promo man hooked them up with Wein, a legendary impresario known for developing the Newport Jazz and Folk Festivals. The Cleveland date also appealed to Mike Belkin's taste.

Belkin Productions Presents In Cleveland

DAVID BOWIE

AND THE SPIDERS FROM MARS

★ *In His First U.S. Appearance* ★

FRIDAY SEPTEMBER 22 – 8:30 PM
CLEVELAND MUSIC HALL

$4.50 Advance – All Seats Reserved – Mail Order Only

Send check or money order payable to BELKIN PRODUCTIONS and mail to
DAVID BOWIE 1220 E. 6th St, Cleveland, Ohio 44114 with self addressed stamped envelope

Belkin Productions brought David Bowie to Cleveland for his first US tour.

"I like jazz," says Belkin, who used to visit such long-gone Cleveland jazz haunts as Moe's Main Street at Euclid Avenue and East 79th Street, and Lindsay's Sky Bar at Euclid and East 106th. He and his high school friends would go on Sundays when bars would allow them in even though they were under age. In the late 1950s and early 1960s, jazz was popular, Belkin says, conjuring an era when East 105th Street and its environs were effectively Cleveland's uptown entertainment district. (Belkin was fond of other forms of amusement. This sometimes bad boy would from time to time skip school to catch the burlesque queens at the Roxy, a striptease theater on East 9th Street next to Jean's Fun House.)

In a deal arranged by WJW, the Belkins agreed to invest $25,000 (a significant sum, about $190,000 in 2017 dollars) in Wein's Ohio Jazz Festival-North, starring bop keyboard virtuoso Horace Silver, soul organist Jimmy Smith, the Dave Brubeck Quartet, vocalists Sarah Vaughan and Joe Williams, and trumpeter Miles Davis. Jules suggests in the *Pollstar* video interview that they borrowed from the family clothing business to enter the deal with Wein. It was a big risk and big money for the time. And for a while, the outlook wasn't great for a couple of reasons.

First, tickets were priced at $3.50, $4.50, $5.50, and $6 for box seats, an aggressive schedule for those times, and they were available at Richman Brothers clothing stores and Burrows (a local chain selling books and office supplies). But while sales were sluggish, anxiety among the promoters was high. About a week before the show, the Belkins decided to check out the Richman Brothers in downtown Cleveland. As they arrived, their anxiety turned to surprise when they saw a line of customers outside; something unusual was going on. Turns out fans were finally buying tickets for that jazz show because they had money in hand—and the Belkins were delighted.

But legitimate concerns about the concert remained. The show was booked into the old Cleveland Arena for August 6, 1966. The concert venue was just a short distance from the Hough neighborhood, the site of deadly and destructive riots that received national coverage for the stunning visuals resulting from arson, ardent protests, and Ohio National Guard troops in full uniform— and tanks rolling through neighborhoods. The riots lasted from July 18-23, and less than two weeks later, nerves were frayed and tension was high. What would the atmosphere be like at the concert?

George Wein, left, chats with WJW's late night host, Dave Hawthorne, at the Ohio Valley Jazz Festival.

As a contemporary jazz show, it was expected to draw an integrated audience. The day of the show, the Cleveland summer evening was a particularly steamy one, and there was no air conditioning at the Cleveland Arena. Some 8,000 fans crowded into the decrepit venue at 36th Street and Euclid Avenue for the sellout show. While the arena was "broken down, the show went off big time, with a mixed audience of black and white," Belkin says. "It was a big success in spite of the Hough riots." The venue finally closed in 1974 and was demolished in 1977.

The agreement with Anderson and Wein stipulated that if the date made money, "it would be divided 50 percent to George Wein and 50 percent to Belkin & Anderson, and the split with Anderson and Belkin of the other 50 percent would be equal," Belkin says. The profit was $5,000, so Wein and Belkin & Anderson each got $2,500; Anderson got $1,250, the brothers $625 each.

That jazz date was an inflection point for the Belkins' promotion business. Belkin says he had little to do with that seminal jazz show.

From left, Jules Belkin, Johnny Carson, Mike Belkin and Mrs. Downs.

Jules handled the advertising and, with Wein, did the accounting. Yet Mike still relishes its success.

"I remember that the crowd was very excited, and being partners with George Wein, who was and is a jazz icon, meant that this was the big time," he says. "George was the king of jazz." Wein and his public relations officer, Dino Santangelo, did most of the heavy lifting at that show, Belkin says.

It was the first show to make Mike and Jules real money but ironically, it was the last with Anderson as a partner. After that, it was Belkin Productions all the way. No intrigue or acrimony though, as the parting with Anderson was more than amicable. "Anderson said, 'look, guys, we went through two cancellations, and we didn't make any money...' He finally made some money," Belkin says. "He said to us that night, guys, how about you both own the whole thing?" And

Anderson left the concert business; he gave the Belkins his half and set them on their own because "he was so happy he finally was part of a major show that made some money," Belkin says.

After the success of Wein's mini jazz festival, the Belkins moved from the men's clothing store into their own office catty corner from the store, in a bank building also on West 25th Street, and hired their first staffer, administrative secretary Carla Scheck. They were about to hit the big time—at least the bigger time.

They presented several other shows in 1966, but Belkin productions really hit its stride in 1967. That also was the year they solidified the relationships that would give them such power for decades.

In 1967, they presented at least 14 shows including ones by the Four Seasons in Columbus and Youngstown and Andy Williams in Dayton. Another of those 1967 concerts was on February 9, when they presented the Supremes at Music Hall, capitalizing on the hot Motown label. The Supremes sold out, despite competition from the Royal Winnipeg Ballet at Public Auditorium, a February 5 offering by another promoter.

Another sellout came on April 14, when Belkin Productions presented Norman Granz's Jazz at the Philharmonic at Music Hall featuring Duke Ellington and Ella Fitzgerald. "Music Hall was a great place to play," says Belkin, noting the brothers presented New Orleans trumpeter Al Hirt there on February 19 after they had produced him in Cincinnati the night before. Belkin Productions was getting busier—more shows, of different types and in different venues and different Midwest cities.

They also booked more traditional acts, challenging the operations of other promoters. They presented Frank Sinatra in his Cleveland debut at Public Auditorium on July 6. Meanwhile, Musicarnival, that tent theater in Warrensville Heights, presented Johnny Mathis for five days that July, Wayne Newton that July 5-9 and Simon and Garfunkel that July 30. Musicarnival primarily presented Broad-

LINER NOTES..................

Working My Way Back to Youngstown

Frankie Valli of the Four Seasons has played Northeast Ohio many times over 55 years. In that time, Mike Belkin and Valli have developed a lasting friendship. However, their first gig together could have ended in tragedy.

Valli and the band were staying at a hotel in Cleveland; the show was in Youngstown, near the Pennsylvania line. Belkin and Valli, only a year apart in age, struck up a mutual admiration immediately, sharing an interest in fashion and clothes. Belkin offered to show Valli the clothing store he was still managing in Ashtabula, northeast of Cleveland. The young men decided they had time to make the 60-mile trip before the show—even though it was starting to snow.

"It was snowing heavily on the drive out to Ashtabula," recalls Belkin of the 60-mile drive along Lake Erie, infamous for its traffic-crippling, "lake effect" snow. Finally arriving, they parked the car and went into the store. However, the two were nervous about getting to the Youngstown venue to make curtain call, let alone the sound check.

"The drive from Ashtabula to Youngstown is not a short drive, either," Belkin continues, since none of the route was freeway in 1967.

After a white-knuckle drive through the snow-drifted countryside, Belkin managed to get the frontman to the show on time. "I was very, very relieved that Frankie and I were still alive," he sighs, 50 years later. Despite this dangerous wintry escapade, Valli and the Four Seasons still allowed Belkin to promote 30 shows over the next few decades—sun, rain, sleet or snow.

way-type shows in competition with the Kenley Players. Eventually, it also presented Led Zeppelin on July 20, 1969, on a $4 bill with Grand Funk Railroad, beating Belkin to the booking. Belkin wasn't happy about losing that booking, and his competitive nature wouldn't allow him to be a good loser.

Testing the Waters

Rock 'n' roll was still finding its audience, especially in Cleveland.

In those early years, when the brothers forged the alliances with agents, venues, bands, band managers and the media that made their business so successful, they booked all kinds of acts, from Johnny Carson to Bill Cosby to the Lipizzaner Stallions. Presenting entertainment of mass appeal would figure throughout the life of Belkin Productions; the brothers were flexible when it came to the kind of entertainment they produced, figuring it was OK as long as it sold tickets, and much more than OK when it sold out.

"Where other promoters around the country just stayed with one music or entertainment genre, the Belkins would book anything that could sell a ticket," says Barry Gabel, senior vice president of marketing and promotional sales at Live Nation, the successor to Belkin Productions.

Gabel, a rock 'n' roll dynamo, wasn't in on the beginning, but he became a go-to-guy in the peak years of Belkin Productions—and, like the brothers themselves, played an instrumental role in the evolution of the company to the present in its form as Live Nation. Gabel worked with both brothers and now works with Belkin's son, Live Nation Midwest vice president Michael Belkin. He affirms that Belkin Productions booked not only rock 'n' roll but also acts like the Moscow Circus, the theatrical production "La Cage Aux Folles," the actress Bette Davis, American Gladiator segments, the Big Apple Circus, Cirque du Soleil, and closed-circuit TV boxing (the at-event predecessor to pay-per-view events that would fuel fortunes for boxers, promoters, and cable companies).

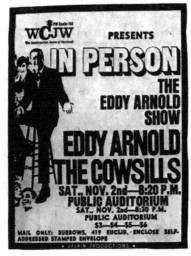

Mike Belkin's date book from October 1968, shows a busy month for the young producer. The acts scheduled certainly illustrate the range of target audience and the ground Belkin Productions covered outside of Cleveland. All of the ads on this page could have been published on the same day and on the same newspaper page, because all the events are referenced in that date book. The Belkin Productions label was fast becoming synonymous with quality live entertainment.

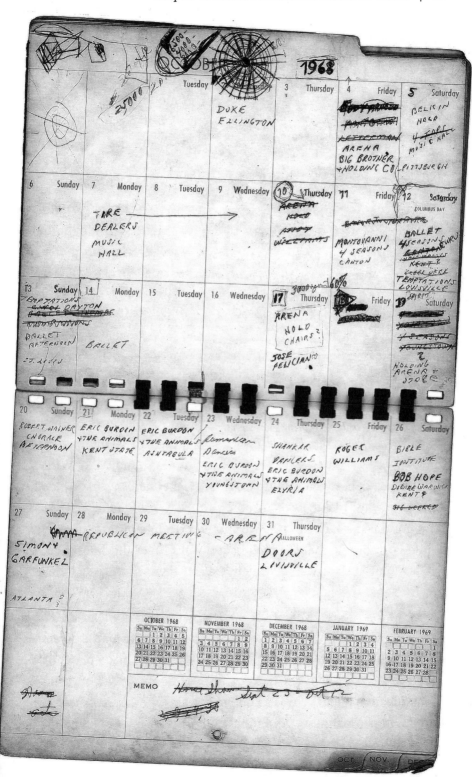

This ad, also from 1968, appears to presage the record-setting World Series of Rock shows at Cleveland Municipal Stadium, since it directs fans to "bring blankets" to Shaker Heights High Football Field.

Mike Belkin hired Gabel in 1979, launching what would by 2017 amount to a 37-year career. It began with Gabel opening Belkin Productions mail, but only two years later, he was deeply involved in marketing.

Even though he viewed the brothers as partners in their business, Gabel says, "Jules and Mike had different interests." At the same time, he suggested, Mike was the idea man. "He was in Ashtabula, he was with the socks, that guy LeRoy was doing these big band jazz things, and Mike went to Jules and said, hey, you want to do this?" Gabel said speculatively, "At least he always included his brother, the way I understand it. Mike then got the spark to say, hey, we should do something. I think Jules would corroborate that. To me it was always Mike and Jules that ran the business." Mike was definitely the brother who created Belkin Productions.

In a broad sense, Mike Belkin was the innovator, his brother the nuts and bolts man who handled a variety of responsibilities. For example, Mike pioneered the practice of charging one ticket price in advance and a higher one the day of show. He doesn't recall quite when he launched that, but it "was a couple of years" after the brothers went into the music business. San Francisco promoter Bill Graham, one of many contemporaries and a close friend, called Belkin to say it was a great idea.

The notion behind it was the drive to cover costs sooner and to get the ticket buyer to make a commitment, explains Belkin. The earlier the customer bought, the better and cheaper the ticket. The idea was to create a loyal following, to stimulate sales, and to "remove any pressure that the ticket buyers would have regarding good seats."

It was Mike's idea to start the Belkin Concert Club, a concept that has been replicated in every venue and fan club. "It was a very interesting concept and I have to pat myself on the back," he says. "It was an absolutely brilliant move, a thought that occurred to me just like the two-price tickets." Mike always had the "last word."

Barry Gabel in 1985.

(After he's patted himself on the back, Belkin jokes that he has to go to the emergency room to get his shoulder relocated.)

The Concert Club membership notion popped into Belkin's mind while he was on vacation in Florida. As he soaked up the sun, Belkin decided he had to come up with something different and interesting, something exclusive. Excited, he phoned the office right away, calling for a meeting as soon as he returned home.

Anybody could join the Concert Club, starting with a $25 membership fee that was annually renewable. That investment got the Club member the best seats to a particular concert. "We rotated the mem-

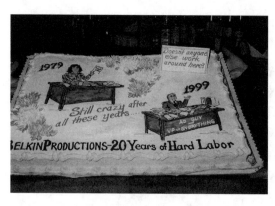

This cake surprised Barry Gabel at a milestone event.

bers so when you got first-row tickets for this show, next show you're not going to get first-row tickets, but you'll still get good tickets," Belkin says. The Concert Club seats were always good—never nosebleed, never back row. "It became a cult thing because everybody wanted to be a member of the Club," says Belkin. "Everybody at some point wants to be in the front row."

And it was young Gabel's responsibility to run the Club. "People joined the Concert Club for a small fee and they would receive a monthly newsletter about shows that were coming to town and they would order tickets through the Concert Club and get preferred ticket locations," Gabel says. "I basically was the customer service frontline person, opened the mail, and facilitated the tickets."

Eventually, though, the Concert Club was a victim of its own success. Belkin Productions had to close down the Club because demand "was so great and we couldn't really keep everyone happy; there weren't enough premium tickets," Gabel says. While the Club was closed, the essential Belkin commitment to create and keep a loyal fan base remained.

The Business Shifts

As their involvement in the music business deepened, the Belkin brothers' interest in the clothing stores diminished. Even with a growing staff, there were limits to their time and attention. They closed their Painesville outlet in 1968, their Ashtabula branch soon after. They kept the store on West 25th Street a bit longer, finally shuttering

LINER NOTES.................

Those Troublesome Doors

In spite of the Doors' controversial nature—or perhaps because of that—the group was also very popular. Their Cleveland-area debut was on September 14, 1967 at Musicarnival, a show that drew only 700 to a tent that could hold 2,500. That show was *not* produced by the Belkins.

When the Doors returned to play Cleveland's Public Auditorium on August 3, 1968, the Belkins were involved and the place sold out. According to Doorshistory.com, lead singer Jim Morrison jumped into the audience during "Light My Fire," driving the fans crazy.

Following a canceled show at Public Auditorium set for March 29, 1969, the band was booked for consecutive nights at the Allen Theatre February 13-14, 1970. Mike Belkin was hoping the first night would go smoothly, as he had plans to camp out with his son, Michael, after the show.

"I was nervous the whole show; police lined the side of the stage and I couldn't wait until the show was over," Belkin recalls. "There were people standing up and they wanted people to sit down and finally they ended the show, and I went, 'Oh, my God, it's over with no problems,' because no one knew what was going to happen."

The band left the stage but Morrison came back out by himself. "People were already starting to leave and they all rushed back into the auditorium," said Belkin, who badly wanted the show to be over. But it wasn't.

"They did a couple more songs, then they went off, then the police came out, and lined up (along) the entire front of the stage. It's not like people were rushing the stage and causing problems; I'm thinking, 'Oh God, now what? Is this going to cause a problem?'"

But it didn't, and Belkin went backstage to thank the Doors, "telling them, 'I'm sorry I can't spend time with you because I have to go to my son's sleepover.'"

LINER NOTES.................

Do Not Disturb

Mike Belkin was invited for dinner at Playboy founder Hugh Hefner's Chicago mansion after a Doors show at Chicago Auditorium Theater on June 14, 1969. Also on hand: The Doors. Missing in a different kind of action: Jim Morrison.

"We had a very nice dinner," Belkin recalls. "Hugh Hefner was there, and toward the end of the dinner we noticed that Jim Morrison had disappeared, nowhere to be found. So we were concerned that he wasn't around. We asked some of the girls to go upstairs; we weren't allowed to do that, so we thought they could learn if he might by chance be up there. They went upstairs and came back down. He wasn't there, either."

The hunt for Morrison intensified. "Where could he be? We went downstairs where the pool was and there were separate rooms off the swimming pool; we just went from room to room, flicking on the lights. There were double bunks in each room and we kept flicking on lights. We finally flicked on the light at the end and there he was, and he was having a wonderful time with one of the Playboy bunnies. I just flipped the light back off and we went back up to the dining room. Later that evening, we went back to the hotel. But I don't think Jim Morrison left the mansion that night."

it in 1972. By that time, they were firmly entrenched in the rock 'n' roll business.

In the later '60s, they co-promoted with WIXY, the legendary Top 40 station. But in the '70s, WMMS-FM, Malrite Communications' Cleveland juggernaut and a frequent partner with the Belkins, came to rule the city's airwaves, supplanting its AM predecessor.

The Belkins were tight with Norman Wain, Joe Zingale and Bob Weiss, founders of WIXY 1260. "We were with WIXY an awful lot," says Belkin. "They were important to the success of Belkin Productions," particularly after it separated from Anderson and went on its own. The considerations in that alliance, and in later ones with WMMS 100.7, *Scene* magazine, Budweiser and others, were promotional, not financial. The Belkins kept their business private, confining it to family. "We never had any partners in the business," says Belkin, noting he and Jules were sole owners of Belkin Productions. "Just to have any partner for the sake of having one is not the best thing."

They also would co-promote when they stepped outside their Cleveland base. In Pittsburgh, their partner was Pat DeCesare, whose partner was Rich Engler; in Detroit they partnered with, among others, Maurice Downs, who was tight with Aretha Franklin. They partnered with Ron Delsener in New York City, Connecticut and New Jersey; Delsener also was the main owner of the Savoy, a New York club Mike and Jules had a sliver of in the early '80s. And they co-promoted closed-circuit boxing matches with New York-based Cedric Kushner. Their partner in the Indianapolis area was Dave Lucas of Sunshine Productions. They co-promoted with Bill Graham Presents in northern California. Their Boston partner was Don Law and their Wisconsin counterpart was Herb Frank.

Agents seeking a Cleveland date would contact Mike, telling him which artists they had on tour. "A lot of agents were slippery back then," he says, noting they would call him and his competitors as they were shopping around for the best deal. "As time went on, money was still important but what was just as or even more important was that they got a professional promoter to produce the date so the artist would be happy with the production," he says. One agent who understood this was Frank Barsalona, founder of Premier Talent Agency and representative of the Who, Mike's favorite group.

"Together Mike and Jules were incredibly savvy businessmen," Gabel says. "They were not showy. They were about the business, about making the band happy. They were about being professional with every touch point: the advertising, the buildings, the agents, the managers, the artists. They were about being professional and making sure at the end of the day that the person buying the ticket would feel safe, see a phenomenal show and get home. At the end of the day, that's what made the Belkin name."

Gabel went broad and deep in the Belkin business mix, first with the Concert Club and, starting in 1981, as marketing director, a much more demanding position. He took that over when Jim Marchyshyn left Belkin Productions to be marketing director for WMMS, Malrite Communications' powerful Cleveland outlet. "When I became the marketing guy in '81, Mike was doing other things within the company and Jules was doing the advertising part," says Gabel. So when he took over marketing, he began to work more closely with Jules. "Anybody younger who was part of Mike's world that we were promoting, that was my job," he says. "That's how I worked with both of them."

Despite his business acumen, Belkin has been wrong. Known for being tight with a buck, that attitude has sometimes cost the Belkins. Mike recalls, "There was a Pink Floyd tour that was going out on the road and the agent had called me to let me know there was a date available in Cleveland and how much the guarantee would be." The guarantee refers to the fee the promoter pays the band, not including expenses for lights and sound, staging, food, everything that surrounds a concert. A guarantee is computed against a percentage of gross ticket sales. Whichever is higher is what the bands get paid.

"I thought that (the guarantee) was outrageously high and I got into a verbal fight with the agent," Belkin says. "I was not yelling and

LINER NOTES.................

Keeping out of Trouble

Mike Belkin knows when to butt out, a valuable attribute for someone who regularly deals with celebrities. At one point, he was in charge of a tour featuring Liza Minnelli, meeting her and her agent in whatever city she was playing.

"Prior to one show, she wanted to rest and it was a sold-out show," Belkin recalls. Tours can be exhausting and Minnelli needed down time. Minnelli, who at that time was dating a man connected to the television industry, was eventually able to do the out-of-town show that night.

Her man came to the show, "and I think they had a disagreement and he was going around knocking on doors trying to find her," Belkin says. "I'm in my room, and I hear out in the hallway someone pounding on doors and I wasn't about to go out and see what was going on."

Belkin let the incident die down. "I wasn't going to insert myself into a disagreement between Liza and her guy," he says.

screaming, but I was quite vociferous in the conversation, and I didn't get the date. It went to a different promoter. What happened was I was taught a lesson. The lesson was you don't burn bridges—because as a result, we didn't get a date for Pink Floyd for two years." Pink Floyd toured behind "Dark Side of the Moon" in 1972, playing the Allen Theatre that April 25. It would play several more Cleveland dates,

WIXY

Presents

IN PERSON

the SUPREMES

Plus All Star Show

FEB. 9th - MUSIC HALL

8:00 P.M.

$4-$5-$6 Tickets on sale now

BURROWS—419 EUCLID

And all branch stores

A BELKIN PRODUCTION

This February, 1967 ad from The Cleveland Press promotes one of the many WIXY/Belkin shows.

including a World Series of Rock milestone.

Meanwhile, the Belkins were spreading their brand. "We hooked up with a radio station or TV in practically every concert that we did, because we were looking to get more bang for the buck," says Belkin. "The big thing with the radio stations is that they would do 'WIXY 1260 and Belkin Presents'— that was important for them, to get their call letters out. Because they're going to sell time for whatever there is, they want potential advertisers to hear their name. That was always very, very important for us.

"Our strategy was to advertise relentlessly, so we also advertised in print, which was newspapers," he says. "Back then it was the (Cleveland) *Press* and the *Plain Dealer*. Ultimately, we made very big deals with the PD where they would be a co-sponsor, but not an investor. In return for them putting an ad in their newspaper, they would print 'The Cleveland Plain Dealer and Belkin Productions Present,'" generating publicity and an aura of hipness.

Keeping Ahead of the Trend

Timing is everything, and the Belkins' timing was right on the money. It all came together for them—and for the region—through rock 'n' roll, which began as countercultural phenomenon, then went mainstream, even corporate. The Belkins were ahead of the curve, particularly early on. "I knew there was a void in the market and we were willing to take a chance," says Mike. "I saw a trend developing"

Rock 'n' roll was on the ascent, and Motown, in particular, "was very hot."

They started during the heyday of Top 40 radio, when Cleveland AM powerhouses like WIXY, WKYC, WGAR and WJW were not only competitive, they had marketing clout. As the '60s gave way to the '70s, however, FM took hold, ending the singles era by way of album rock.

Record companies were discovering the 18-to-34 demographic and figured out how to sate its appetite—with vinyl. "Music-wise, you really had to have a record deal, otherwise you couldn't get played on the radio," says Belkin. Artists needed album deals, and album deals were being made. The rock 'n' roll business was beginning to boom, and not only musically. It brought with it associated commerce like Daffy Dan's T-shirts, record stores on virtually every corner, record sections in department stores, celebrity DJs, and fans who got hooked on rock as kids and never grew out of it.

There were clubs, too, even club mini-chains, like the Hullabaloos in Cleveland's suburbs, and the Piccadilly and Otto's Grotto downtown. And there was the Agora franchise Henry LoConti launched in Little Italy in February 1966, just after the Belkins debuted with that Four Freshmen-New Christy Minstrels concert.

The Belkins always had their eyes on the national prize: big-name acts, whether rock 'n' rollers like the Who and the Rolling Stones or, early on, TV stars like Johnny Carson and Sonny & Cher. They also kept their eye on local and emerging talent, showcasing bands that looked like they might break out. "We always did local acts, but in the beginning, there were clubs, and Hank LoConti was doing that stuff back then, smaller stuff," Belkin says. "That caliber of artist that used to play in the clubs, if they did good business I offered them the potential to play at a legitimate theater." Bands had to prove themselves "unless it was some kind of hot talent like a Springsteen," he says.

By the '70s, Belkin Productions was on solid ground as the key promoter in Cleveland. The Belkin empire was striking gold, and the characters with whom the brothers interacted had stories of their own to tell. As for Mike Belkin, he was starting to redefine his role, shifting focus from concert booking and production to management and the record business itself.

Chapter 5

Goodbye '60s, Hello '70s

Too many things to do
Too many words to talk
Moments too few

James Gang ~ *Take A Look Around*

By the 1970s, Belkin Productions was a major promoter throughout the Midwest, and Mike Belkin was happy—but he started getting itchy. A man who can't sit still and a man with a deep work ethic, Belkin was eager to branch out into artist management, to spread his professional wings.

Turns out he and his main clients did quite well with each other.

Belkin's first signing was the James Gang. The second was Michael Stanley, the third Donnie Iris and the Cruisers. Each band is strongly identified with its home: the Gang and Stanley with Cleveland, Iris and the Cruisers with Pittsburgh. Each, too, enjoyed popularity beyond their own region.

Belkin managed other acts including guitarist Mason Ruffner (on whose debut album Cruiser keyboard player-songwriter Mark Avsec played), the Sir Douglas Quintet with Doug Sahm, Breathless (also featuring Avsec) and the Staple Singers. He also managed Wild Cherry, a group formed by Mingo Junction man Rob Parissi, writer of the wildly successful tune, "Play That Funky Music." Avsec and Iris also played in the Wild Cherry touring band. The interconnections were endless and remain so, a hallmark of the business in general and Belkin associates particularly.

Belkin has a soft spot for the James Gang, the Michael Stanley Band and other Stanley configurations, and Donnie Iris and the Cruisers. "I was very fortunate to be able to manage these bands, particularly because I love the guys personally," he says. "Which I think is so important; it's tough to give heartfelt advice to someone you don't feel that close to."

The James Gang, Stanley, and Donnie Iris and the Cruisers value their relationships with Belkin and have been steady clients and friends. The Stanley and Iris groups regularly sell out shared bills in Cleveland and Pittsburgh, and Belkin always goes to those shows.

Each band has had its share of ups and downs, but judging the overall success of the Gang, the Michael Stanley Band and Iris and the Cruisers is a challenging and perhaps pointless exercise. After all, much depends on how you define the term "success." When it comes to the Gang and MSB, for example, it's the difference between being a big fish in a big pond and a big fish in a small pond. Both the Gang and Stanley made more than a regional mark, but the Gang went far wider: Belkin helped that group go national, even international. At the same time, MSB set a record as the most popular group in Cleveland history in 1982 with four sellout nights at Blossom Music Center in Cuyahoga Falls: that August 25-26 and 30-31, it drew a total of

74,404. Then, unfortunately largely due to record company politics, the band's ascent stalled. MSB soldiered on until finally disbanding in 1987.

While Jim Fox, Dale Peters and Joe Walsh have occasionally re-united as the classic James Gang—the last time was in 2006—Stanley, Iris and the Cruisers have been playing steadily, Stanley with the Ghost Poets and the Resonators, Iris with the Cruisers.

The James Gang

Drummer Jimmy Fox played briefly in the Outsiders, a Cleveland group most famous for its 1966 Top 5 hit, "Time Won't Let Me." Although Fox launched the James Gang in 1966, it took a while to settle into its most potent configuration with bassist Peters and superstar guitarist Joe Walsh. The James Gang peaked in the early 1970s, then lost its guitar star and sputtered out in 1977. Belkin entered the picture

The James Gang in 1971: Jimmy Fox, from left, Dale Peters and Joe Walsh.

Mike Belkin's new date book: a larger size for a busier promoter.

when the Gang was at its zenith and about to go into decline. Yet he stuck with them.

Fox, Peters and Walsh met as students at Kent State in the late 1960s. Walsh left Kent for good after May 4, 1970, when the Ohio

1971

FRIDAY · 1st A²
SANTANA - CINCI
CHUCK BERRY - NEW ORLE...

SATURDAY · 2nd

SUNDAY · 3rd
GORDON LIGHTFOOT
CLEVE.
SANTANA - CLEVE

THURSDAY · 7th
JAMES TAYLOR - OHIO UNIV.
J.C. SUPERSTAR - BUCKNELL
· SYRACUSE

FRIDAY · 8th m⁻ᵗ
JAMES TAYLOR - MICHIGAN ST.
J.C. SUPERSTAR - BUCKNELL

SATURDAY · 9th
BELKIN-A
TRAFFIC
CLEVE.
J.C. SUPERSTAR
ROCHESTER

SUNDAY · 10th
GRAND FUNK
CINCI
JAMES TAYLOR
UNIV. OF WISCONSIN
J.C. SUPERSTAR
ROCHESTER
ALICE COOPER
RICHMOND, VA.

THURSDAY · 14th

FRIDAY ·' 15th
FOUR SEASONS - CLEVE
NEIL DIAMOND - MADISON

SATURDAY · 16th
BELKIN-A
JAZZ FESTIVAL
CLEVE.
FOUR SEASONS
YOUNGSTOWN

SUNDAY · 17th
M POCO
CINCI

THURSDAY · 21st A o.m. ▾
J.C. SUPERSTAR
LACROSSE, WISC
J.C. SUPERSTAR - AKRON

FRIDAY · 22nd A o.m. ▾
J.C. SUPERSTAR - CINC

SATURDAY · 23rd
A o.m. ▾
RASCALS
MEMORIAL
AUDITORIUM COLI...
J.C. SUPERSTAR
CINC

SUNDAY · 24th
A r.m. ▾
J.C. SUPERSTAR
YOUNGSTOWN

THURSDAY · 28th A o.m. ▾
J.C. SUPERSTAR
DETROIT

FRIDAY · 29th A o.m. ▾
GRATEFUL DEAD - CLEVE.

SATURDAY · 30th
BELKIN · A
GRAND FUNK
CLEVE.

SUNDAY · 31st
A ·

THURSDAY · **FRIDAY** · **SATURDAY** · **SUNDAY**

1971 JULY 1971	1971 AUGUST 1971	1971 SEPTEMBER 1971	1971 OCTOBER 1971	1971 NOVEMBER 1971	1971 DECEMBER 1971
S M T W T F S	S M T W T F S	S M T W T F S	S M T W T F S	S M T W T F S	S M T W T F S
1 2 3	1 2 3 4 5 6 7	1 2 3 4	1 2	1 2 3 4 5 6	1 2 3 4
4 5 6 7 8 9 10	8 9 10 11 12 13 14	5 6 7 8 9 10 11	3 4 5 6 7 8 9	7 8 9 10 11 12 13	5 6 7 8 9 10 11
11 12 13 14 15 16 17	15 16 17 18 19 20 21	12 13 14 15 16 17 18	10 11 12 13 14 15 16	14 15 16 17 18 19 20	12 13 14 15 16 17 18
18 19 20 21 22 23 24	22 23 24 25 26 27 28	19 20 21 22 23 24 25	17 18 19 20 21 22 23	21 22 23 24 25 26 27	19 20 21 22 23 24 25
25 26 27 28 29 30 31	29 30 31	26 27 28 29 30	24₃₁ 25 26 27 28 29 30	28 29 30	26 27 28 29 30 31

National Guard killed four students protesting President Richard M. Nixon's bombing of Cambodia.

The Gang took a few years to coalesce. One of its earliest incarnations featured the stunning guitarist Glenn Schwartz, who left to record an immortal solo on Pacific Gas & Electric's "Are You Ready?" and its first album featured Tom Kriss on bass. But Kriss

LINER NOTES...............

Everybody up Against the Wall

Mike Belkin's old friend, the legendary San Francisco promoter Bill Graham, threw a very theatrical scare into Belkin and other music moguls on April 22, 1968. The occasion was a meeting of the International Promoters Association on Long Island.

"The reason for the meeting was trying to have everybody work with each other," says Belkin. "The meeting was at a hotel, we had lunch there, and the reason we really had the meeting was because Bill Graham was offering artists deals to give him all their dates nationwide.

"He wasn't invited to the meeting but he was aware of it. There were about 22 of us. So what happened is that we were having the meeting and Bill Graham burst in, along with two guys with machine guns who were dressed like hoods, and broke up the meeting."

It was a joke, and Graham, who died in a plane crash in 1991, began to work with fellow promoters in the cities where they were based. "Bill was a good friend," says Belkin.

left, and the next two studio recordings and a live one featured Peters on that instrument.

Of Belkin's major clients, the Gang hit first and faded first. Walsh joined shortly after Schwartz left, but didn't stay in the Gang long enough to perpetuate its success. It peaked in the early 1970s as one of the original power trios; Walsh, Belkin's favorite guitarist, also is a favorite of The Who's Pete Townshend (another Belkin rave). The definitive Gang toured hard from 1969 through 1971, when Walsh left to form Barnstorm with Canton drummer Joe Vitale and bassist Kenny Passarelli. Walsh's departure left a wound that wouldn't heal; Fox says it hurt the Gang much like the death of drummer Keith Moon in 1978 hurt the Who. But Belkin credits Walsh for the band's initial success. Both "Rides Again" and "Thirds" went gold, signifying album sales of at least a half-million each.

Still, even after Joe Walsh's departure, the Gang kept on, employing various singers and guitarists until "Jesse Come Home," its final album, in 1976.

The Gang's business history is complicated. At least it was before Belkin stepped in. Until then, the Gang was managed by Mark Barger, and in 1968 the group secured a record label deal with ABC Dunhill. (Barger also managed the Lemon Pipers, a one-hit wonder from Oxford, Ohio known for the classic tune, "Green Tambourine.")

How the Gang hooked up with Belkin is a story in itself. It's largely told by Fox, who would go on to work for Belkin Productions, Sweet City—the custom record label Belkin founded with Carl Maduri—and Belkin himself.

"I literally walked down the street (to Barger's office) one day and said, how would you like to manage a band?" Fox recalls of the Barger pact. Barger said fine, but the relationship soured because, as Fox suggests, management was "chemically compromised." The terms were bad, too. The Gang wanted out, so Fox sought out Belkin, who says they felt his standing as a major promoter in the concert business would serve them better than Barger.

Fox says Belkin wasn't willing to take the group under his wing until it had a record contract. "I went to Belkin first; Mike basically said to me, come back when you have a record deal, and he said it in a nice way," says Fox. "I called him a number of times and he wouldn't even take my call. He was the promoter, but he wasn't known as an artist manager."

Belkin finally picked up the phone when Fox told him he was sitting with Fox's cousin, Sid Meisel, whom Belkin knew from Cleveland Heights High School. Meisel turned Fox onto jazz. More critically, Meisel used to play basketball with Belkin at Heights High. Personal bond established, Fox told Belkin the Gang wanted out of its current record deal.

"He said, come on in, we came in and talked, I showed him the contract, said we got to get out of this deal, it's a terrible deal, and he agreed. So he went to work getting us out of the management contract and getting an improved contract with ABC. It cost us, of course; it's never free." But Belkin did what he said he would, signing his first band to a three-year management contract in 1969. He also signed Fox, Peters and Walsh to personal contracts with the same term.

With "Yer' Album" about to be released on the short-lived ABC Bluesway label, along with Belkin management, "all of a sudden for the first time we felt as if we had someone speaking for us who was capable," Fox says. (As producer and engineer, Bill Szymczyk would become a major force with the Gang and a stalwart of Michael Stanley's.)

"I would get X percent for managing them, which meant being involved with the record company and trying to get them to do more for the band," Belkin recalls. It also meant booking the Gang for dates and personal appearances, such as record store signings. Belkin also vowed to get the three a better record deal—with ABC, at least at first.

Ganging up

The Gang started small, working clubs and high schools and graduation parties, establishing a reputation as "a kick-ass rock 'n'

Jimmy Fox in 1971.

roll trio," says Belkin. "The record company loved them because they would be selling records. But ABC never did enough, never really got behind the band like they should have. It was very frustrating for me."

Fox also recognized the advantage Belkin might have when it came to booking. "We just took it for granted that was part of the benefit of having a manager who also promoted concerts," he says.

Belkin "drove a hard bargain, it meant he wanted to win," says Fox. "That's why the band never held his toughness against him; they viewed it as an asset because he was doing it in one sense for us. He may have been doing it for himself, but he was doing it for us, too. That's what you want in a manager—a manager who will fight for you. And I believe that Mike did that."

As the 1960s turned into the '70s, the Belkin brothers would confer "as to the artist and artist's fee, and if we both agreed on the band, which we most often did, then Jules would do the booking," Belkin says. "We shared everything: the dollars in the booking and the dollars in the management. It was all 50-50 from day one, win, lose or draw."

Belkin, who by that time had cultivated promoters in other parts of the region, says that when the Gang had an open date, "rather than not working I would try and sell the date to another promoter in another city if that made sense money-wise and mileage-wise."

By the time he took over Gang management, the trio was doing quite well, regularly selling out clubs all over Ohio and into New York State. But despite that year's release of its debut, it hadn't quite broken out. Then everything changed.

In an interview with ultimateclassicrock.com celebrating the 45th anniversary of the "James Gang Rides Again" album, bassist Peters says, "We were doing real well in the clubs, and you could do that back then. You could show up at a club and put 700 people in, just jammed to the rafters. When I knew things were different, we played somewhere in Pennsylvania, maybe Beaver Falls—some college—and we played at the field house, and I think we had a $1,500 guarantee against the door. The guy expected a thousand people, and that would have been a good crowd for back then. When we showed up, there were 7,000 people. And it was like, 'Who are they here to see?' To me, that was the gig that turned everything. After that, we were surprised at how well we started doing, quickly." Neither Fox nor Peters could supply further details, but that one show speaks loudly.

Making an Impression

In Belkin's view, however, things changed for the bigger and better on October 26, 1969, when the Gang played the Syria Mosque in Pittsburgh. It opened for The Who, Belkin's favorite band, which was featuring material from "Tommy," its first rock opera.

The Who on tour in Europe in 1971.

"It was the turning point," says Belkin. "Pete Townshend heard Walsh play and came out of the dressing room and stood at the side of the stage and listened to the rest of the James Gang. He was so enamored with them that he spoke with his manager and his manager spoke with me and said Townshend wanted to have the James Gang open up for the Who on their English tour."

Belkin arranged the Who-James Gang bill to ABC's satisfaction. The British tour was in October 1970, a European tour the following July. Fox recalls problems with power compatibility may have scuttled the first date, at a place he says was called The Speakeasy (the whocollection.com website says the first date of the Who's 1970 UK tour was The Sophia Gardens in Cardiff, Wales). Whatever the venue, plugs from the United States didn't fit British outlets, but Fox didn't realize that until the Gang got there.

In 1971, the Gang headlined dates in Paris, Amsterdam, and Frankfurt; Belkin, who usually managed from home, was there. The record company arranged the dates, accommodations and transpor-

LINER NOTES.................

Taking Care of Aretha

In the 1970s, Belkin Productions booked an Aretha Franklin date in a co-promotion with Franklin's agency. The contact there was a man we'll call Booker, who was exclusively responsible for Franklin's wants.

Booker offered Mike Belkin the use of his Detroit apartment one night. The two were friends; in fact, Belkin invited Booker and his wife to a Johnny Carson show he produced. But when he got to Booker's place, he discovered another side to the guy. When Belkin opened a door to a closet there and found two rifles, he closed that door fast.

The night before, when Booker picked up Belkin and his brother at the airport, the Detroit man asked whether he could make a quick stop on the way into town. "We said sure, that's fine," Belkin recalls.

"Someone had told us that Booker was involved with the numbers; that's what we knew. Anyway, he stopped at a bar, we waited in the car and he came back out, got in the car and dropped us off at the apartment," Belkin says. "He was the sharpest dresser you'd ever want to see. Whatever suit he had on, it was always a beautiful suit. And he'd match it up with alligator shoes. We got along with him.

"Ultimately, we found out that he wasn't just in the numbers. One of our friends in Detroit called and said, a couple of years later, that he'd send a copy of the front page. " The newspaper reported that Booker had been murdered in a drug deal.

"All I can say about Booker, as far as I was concerned, was he was a gentleman's gentleman," says Belkin.

tation. "It went well," he says. "We did TV everywhere." They also did well with numerous in-store promotions.

Not only did the Gang open for the Who on that chilly jaunt around the English countryside, it mounted record promotions in France, the Netherlands and Japan. "Everything was tied into the record company," Belkin says. "(In) Japan, we were like rock stars. They went crazy over the band."

Fox, Peters and Belkin brought their spouses along to Europe for the 1970 tour with the Who. Between gigs, the Foxes and the Belkins spent a few days in Paris. The French digs were surely better than their London accommodations.

The Who had installed the Gang at the Hyde Park Towers, "the funkiest place I had ever stayed in my life," says Fox. "I can describe it by saying the bathroom was the size that you could perform all functions normal in a bathroom without moving an inch. The bed was like a single bed for myself and my wife. We were on our honeymoon. At 4 in the morning, I get an elbow and my wife says, why did you open the window? I'm freezing. And I say I didn't open the window.

The window that the frame fell out of in the hotel wall in London.

She says, look, the curtains are closing. So I get up and walk over to the window, which frame and all is lying on the ground three stories down. It fell out of the hotel. I complained to Mike. I'm sure the word got back to the Who this wasn't a good place for the future."

As management deals with typical challenges like these, it also has its rewards, especially with a band at its peak. Belkin and Fox say it was a blast to tour with the Who. As they drove from town to town on that career-changing British tour, Fox rode with Who drummer Moon, Walsh with Townshend, and Peters with bassist John Entwistle. (Belkin has a custom pair of leather pants he got through Entwistle, who introduced Belkin to his personal tailor.)

So who sat alongside vocalist Roger Daltrey? "We took turns," Fox says.

This was more than 45 years ago, when AM radio was just giving way to FM and Top 40 singles were still strong but album rock was rearing its head. Telephones were rotary dial, typewriters were manual, and there was no internet.

Management in the analog era was conversation and documents and personal engagement. "There are two kinds of managers," says Fox. "There are managers who like to be out and the ones who are never out; they prefer to stay at home and take care of business. When you're on the road it's harder to take care of business. When you were riding in an automobile in those days, there was no telephone or computer. Today, your office goes with you." Once a band was on the road, it was out of reach until the next town.

Belkin handled all the travel arrangements. Today, he handles publishing and licensing along with his longtime New York attorney, Larry Lighter. A CPA continues to handle the accounting. "My strength is in the day-to-day management of musicians," he says.

Leave it to Belkin to handle the mundane; let the rock stars play. Not that he didn't enjoy the camaraderie.

*John Entwistle in his home. Belkin and Entwistle became good
friends on the James Gang tour.*

That second European tour, in 1971, found the Gang headlining smaller venues including theaters and clubs, usually with local opening acts.

The Gang was on a roll, if a brief one. By the time it released "James Gang Rides Again," featuring the influential track "Funk #49," Peters had replaced Kriss on bass. That lineup also powered the imaginatively titled "Thirds," a spring 1971 release and the last studio album with Walsh. A live record was issued in December 1971 also featuring him. By that time, Belkin was firmly in the driver's seat for the Gang—but Walsh was on his way to a successful solo career.

"Joe felt that he wanted more out of the musical career than playing with the James Gang, and he had already said something to Jimmy and Dale," says Belkin. "They weren't happy about it. I wasn't happy about it because the band was doing quite well."

LINER NOTES...................

The Water's Fine...

Mike Belkin recalls a very wet Who event in Cleveland in the early 1970s. After a sold-out Public Auditorium date, he and his brother, Jules, took the band to dinner at Captain Frank's, a restaurant that was located on the Ninth Street pier that juts out into Lake Erie. The pier is still there, right next to the Rock and Roll Hall of Fame, which opened in 1995.

"Roger Daltrey showed up. So did Pete Townshend and John Entwistle," Belkin says. "We sat down to eat. Jimmy Fox was there, so in comes Keith Moon and Dale Peters. Keith wore a white T-shirt and white pants."

At least they had been white during the show, but "they were all black and dripping wet, soaked to the skin, drenched," Belkin says. "The water was filthy dirty."

When Belkin asked what had happened, Moon said, "I wanted to go for a swim."

"Dale said, I was walking the pier and happened to see Keith was walking in front of me and he jumped into the water off the pier. That's not just a 3-foot jump, and he couldn't get back out of the water, the pier was way too high. Fortunately, there was a life preserver. Dale threw it in, pulled Keith out.

"Had Dale not been walking along at the time, who knows what could have happened to Keith? He would have drowned for sure."

Power Outage

After Walsh left, "it was never as good," Fox says. "Joe was a unique talent. We failed to replace that unique talent over the years, although we certainly had some great guitarists afterwards." Among those: Dominic Troiano, who left the Gang for the Guess Who, and Tommy Bolin, who left the Gang for Deep Purple.

Walsh asked Belkin to help him put a band together. The result was Barnstorm. Belkin wound up managing this interim Walsh band; at the same time, as the Gang's manager and the personal manager of Peters and Fox, he worked on finding a new guitarist, "trying to keep it going with Jimmy and Dale."

Belkin was in an uncomfortable, even untenable, position.

Enter Irving Azoff, booking Barnstorm as Belkin was managing both Barnstorm and the Gang. Azoff, at the time an agent at Associated Booking, eventually took over Walsh's management, paving the way for his solo career and as a member of the Eagles.

Joe Walsh during the European tour with The Who.

Previously, Azoff and Belkin were partners in promoting rock concerts at Majestic Hills, a former boat house in Lake Geneva, south of Madison, Wisconsin. They presented the James Gang and contemporaries like Bloodrock and Mountain at Vall-O-Will Farms, the formal name of the resort, according to Belkin. The relationship between Azoff and Belkin soured for quite some time because of the Walsh situation. It turned particularly acrimonious after Walsh moved to Colorado, firing Belkin and allying with Azoff. Despite a lingering bitterness, Belkin admires Walsh's singular talents—and continues to get a cut from Walsh's recordings.

Barnstorm recorded only one album, an eponymous release, in 1972. Walsh's next record was a solo effort, 1973's "The Smoker You Drink, The Player You Get," a kind of expanded Barnstorm venture featuring the hit, "Rocky Mountain Way."

Walsh, of course, struck lifetime gold in 1975 when he joined the Eagles, one of Azoff's more powerful clients. Belkin has a sliver of that, too. From the first four albums Walsh did with the Eagles, starting with "Hotel California," Belkin gets "a small percentage of what he made for his part in the recording. It's a piece of a piece of a piece."

That is part of a settlement Belkin won in a $3 million suit he filed against ABC Records, its top executives and Azoff, on charges that ABC refused to deal with him on Walsh's behalf and "destroyed Walsh's faith in him." According to an October 26, 1974, article in *Billboard*, "Azoff is accused of further ruining Belkin's credibility with Walsh. As a result, Belkin alleges he was forced to terminate the relationship in June 1974." The article also notes the management deal Belkin and Walsh signed in July 1969 called for Belkin to receive 20 percent of Walsh's record earnings, 25 percent of publishing and 15 percent of Walsh's other entertainment income. Renewed in December 1971, it was to run through July 1975.

In a 2013 story in the Cleveland *Plain Dealer* about Cleveland rock agent-manager David Spero's interaction with the Eagles, writer Michael Heaton noted, "When the Eagles were inducted into the

The 1975 James Gang, from left: Jim Fox, Richard Shack, Dale Peters and Bubba Keith.

Rock Hall in 1998, drummer and lead vocalist Don Henley thanked Azoff, saying, 'Sure, he's Satan. But he's our Satan.' "

(Fans of rock 'n' roll inbreeding should note that years after Belkin managed Walsh, Spero, the son of "Big 5/Upbeat" TV show impresario Herman Spero, took over that role for about 10 years.)

Litigation over Walsh setting Belkin Personal Management against Azoff's Front Line Management would continue through the 1970s.

Soon after Walsh left, things went downhill for the Gang, with

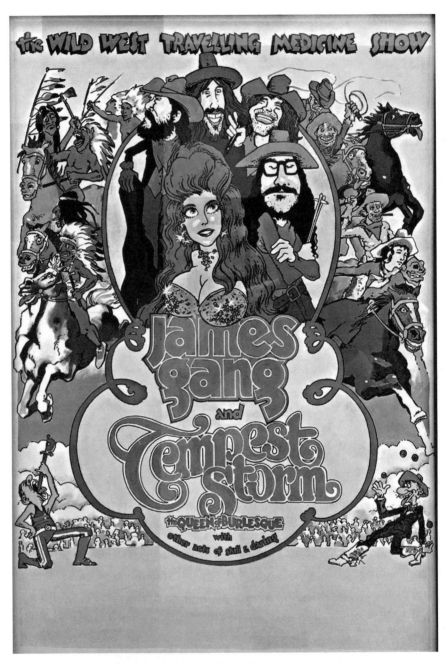

This poster illustrates Belkin's ability to combine diverse acts and make them all work.

fewer dates and smaller paydays. But that development wasn't for Belkin's lack of trying.

While Walsh went on to solo and Eagles success, the Gang "was scrambling," says Belkin. "They got different guitar players and different singers, and their relationship with ABC Dunhill soured. We sued ABC Dunhill. It was the first time that a band really sued a record company for damages. Lack of promotion was the big thing and we said the contract had terminated and they said the James Gang was still under contract."

As that suit, predating the one involving Azoff, wound its way through the courts, Belkin was on the hunt for another label for the Gang and for Walsh, seeking to extricate both from ABC. "My contention was that they were no longer under contract, and I was looking to make a deal elsewhere," he says.

Actually, Walsh was still under contract by way of the original James Gang record contract of 1968, the reason the sole Barnstorm LP was released on ABC Dunhill. The court drama took place in Los Angeles. The plaintiffs ultimately won, freeing the Gang and Walsh to sign with other labels.

Meanwhile, Belkin was courting other labels, including Arista. Label president Clive Davis, who founded Arista in 1974, kept notes of his meetings and telephone calls. Among the latter was a call from ABC Dunhill president Jay Lasker telling Davis the Gang and Walsh were still under contract and ABC Dunhill would sue Arista for interference with an existing agreement if he continued to try to make a deal. Davis sent that threat to Belkin's attorney and the court decided that ABC was unfairly restricting the James Gang and Walsh's abilities to sign with any other company.

Belkin finally won the suit in 1977 when ABC agreed to settle for $1.5 million. After lawyers' fees, the yield for the plaintiffs was about $1 million, according to Belkin. Although a spokesperson for ABC told the *Hollywood Reporter* that the record company would appeal, it never did.

By then, Walsh had long joined the Eagles, just in time to contribute a hard rock sound to "Hotel California," the 1976 album that cemented the band's prominent place in rock history.

The Gang, meanwhile, continued its long, slow slide, going through a number of gifted guitarists and singers like Troiano, Bolin and Roy Kenner before finally disbanding in 1977. It had some fun on its way down, though. Take a unique tour that had just about everything including music, gore and sex appeal, largely thanks to Belkin's creativity.

Now That's Entertainment

Even as a kid, Belkin had a strong sense of theater, a taste he indulged as a kid in his aunts' parlor. Among his most garish promotions was a spring 1973 tour featuring the James Gang, celebrated stripper Tempest Storm, a knife thrower, an illusionist, willing assistants, and Komar.

Under Belkin Personal Management, Belkin signed Storm, whose real name is Annie Banks, to a three-year renewable contract on June 19, 1972. He agreed to pay her a minimum of $2,000 a week, and more if her dates proved more profitable. That signing led to the birth of a singular package featuring "a real burlesque show, with old-time comics, a full revue, dancers and orchestra, all tailored to a college audience," according to Belkin marketing collateral.

Komar stood out because he showed no sign of pain while lying on a bed of nails as a sledgehammer broke a concrete block on his chest. A Wooster, Ohio, man whose real name was Vernon Craig, Komar was a trip, says Fox, who swears Komar could predict the weather.

Komar sounds like a trip indeed. But the spectacle in "Burlesque Goes to College," called the "Wild West Travelling Medicine Show" in a December 23, 1972 *Billboard* brief, was Storm. The tour took place well after Walsh had left, so even though the James Gang was the ostensible headliner, it actually played second fiddle.

In an October 2013 interview with the website mrsrmag.com, the statuesque Storm recalled a particular gig: "One of the most incredible moments in my career was performing in Carnegie Hall in New York. I was working with a group called The James Gang in 1973 and it was six weeks of one-nighters, and I loved it. The big shots thought I was a singer, and then I hit the stage and did my show and they all came back stage for autographs. It was a packed theatre that night!" The date was March 18, 1973.

Tempest Storm in the 1970s.

The unique package Belkin put together scrambled eras, juxtaposing Storm, an ecdysiast extraordinaire, against the James Gang, a heralded rock group trying to stay current. The bill was Belkin's idea. "I created that tour," he says. "To the best of my knowledge, nobody did it before." Where Storm vamped on nostalgia, the Gang was fresh, or at least tried to be.

Colleges surprised Storm, according to an article in the March 13, 1973, Baltimore Evening Sun. She wasn't used to the marijuana smoke, but, she acknowledged, the times were indeed a-changin'.'

"This is a new time," she told a Sun reporter. "I guess new things are happening." What wasn't that happening was the James Gang. As The Sun reported, combining "exotic dancing" with hard rock was a new idea, conceived by Belkin. The tour was more like a rescue mission for the Gang.

"No one thought of it (that combination), seriously at least, until Mike Belkin, the James Gang's manager, decided the group needed something to lift it out of the ordinary, which is where it is marooned," the reporter wrote.

How much Storm displayed varied by venue; at St. Bonaventure University near Buffalo, authorities wouldn't even let her take her coat off. But when she could, no problem. As Belkin told The Associated Press, "Tempest doesn't have a hang-up about showing her chest!"

"Most of the time she was a pleasure," Fox says of Storm. "She was hard on her drummer; she had a live drummer and taped music, so the bumps and grinds were all accented live. But she was very nice to us actually... We traveled together; we were flying commercially in those days... we used to throw fingers among us to see who would carry her wig case. She had a long cylinder thing with her wigs in it.

"It was so much fun to walk with her and see the attention she would get just walking through. She was in her 40s by this time; she was no kid. She had the most extraordinary body I've ever seen. People would see her and literally walk into poles in airport corridors."

Mike Belkin, from left, Sam Belkin, Who vocalist Roger Daltrey, Annie Belkin in the mid-1990s.

Chapter 6

Jumping into the Pool

Show business, baby, it sure is nice...

Michael Stanley Band ~ *Let's Hear It*

Belkin Productions solidified and expanded during the 1970s, when Mike Belkin shifted his focus to management. The company grew, expanding with more staff, geographic reach well beyond Ohio's borders, and diversified concert offerings. One of Belkin Productions' most spectacular innovations was the World Series of Rock, a Mike Belkin idea that fused his interests in entertainment, sports and spectacle.

Belkin Productions was becoming the "go-to" producer for the Midwest, as evidenced in this ad from Scene in 1975.

Even though concerts were already the bread and butter of Belkin Productions, the 1970s also found Belkin managing four bands: Michael Stanley in various configurations; the mega-successful, one-hit wonder Wild Cherry; and Donnie Iris and the Cruisers, kind of an outgrowth of Wild Cherry. He also, of course, managed the James Gang, his first client, until it disbanded in 1977.

Outside of work in the music industry, Belkin was deeply engaged in other life matters. Even as he was actively involved in helping raise his children, Michael and Lisa, Belkin was also navigating the uncertain waters of divorce. After more than 15 years of marriage, Mike and Sue Belkin divorced in 1973. The fact that their divorce was genuinely amicable and respectful helped both Mike and Sue and more importantly, their children. It was critical to both of them that they keep their lives on an even course.

Sue continued living in their Beachwood home with the kids while Mike lived separately, first in an apartment in Willoughby Hills, and later, in 1975 in his current home in Novelty, Ohio. On weekends, Mi-

The monster hit for Cleveland's Sweet City Records.

LINER NOTES...............

Many Years on

"A career is all about loyalty," Elton John said after playing "Candle in the Wind" at the Covelli Centre in Youngstown on May 1, 2010.

John knows a lot about loyalty: His Cleveland debut was a Belkin Production, opening for The Byrds in a sold-out show at Music Hall on November 26, 1970.

Loyalty is the reason John dedicated a new tune he'd written with Leon Russell to Mike Belkin and Michael Belkin, thanking them for promoting him in America ever since his first U.S. tour.

In Youngstown, he gave quite a shoutout to the Belkins, "who've been doing my concerts ever since I came to Ohio ... I think Michael was 2 years old when I first came here ... they've been with me all the way, and I'm really grateful to you guys. Thank you so much."

chael and Lisa would stay over at his home, where he kept two horses for himself plus one for each of the kids. Over the years, a married couple lived on the ground floor, taking care of the horses and doing other housekeeping chores.

The former Sue Belkin married Stan Rubin in 1975. After his divorce, Belkin dated and occasionally lived with woman friends. He was content with his personal life, buoyed by his confidence that his children were on sound footing and that he was rising in the rock 'n' roll business. Still, he would be reminded of the consequences of an unexpected fall, a lesson learned when Belkin discovered that horses and rock 'n' roll don't necessarily mix.

Belkin winces when he recalls what led up to an August 1976 date Elton John played at the Richfield Coliseum. Nearby friends stabled their horses at Belkin's and came over that morning so they could all go for a ride. A pleasant outing turned painful when Belkin's horse spooked when he mounted her. "We met up at the barn and they got on their horses, and I got on my horse. I don't know what freaked my horse out, but she reared, and when a horse rears you want to lean forward, so the reins are loose and the horse doesn't topple backwards. It happened so fast I couldn't react quickly enough, and the horse landed on my left side.

"The horse gets up and I'm on my hands and knees trying to catch my breath," he continues. "My friends were still on their horses and the guy told me I needed to get right back on my horse so I'm not going to be nervous the next time. So I got back on the horse after I caught my breath and was on her for about two minutes. That's when I realized I'm really hurting. I didn't give a shit about getting back on the horse. I'll do it some other time. They took me to the hospital, and I had two broken ribs and I was black and blue from my knee to my groin. I could hardly walk, so they gave me crutches. But I had to work the show that night. Because of my injury, I had to hire a limousine to take me to the show.

"But the show went off great. Elton was fantastic, I did the box office, and I went home. It was just another concert in the life of Mike Belkin."

In addition to occasional bumps like this as well as profound personal changes, Belkin was shifting into high management gear. Michael Stanley, solo and as a band leader, continued to preoccupy him, as did Iris and the Cruisers and, to a lesser extent, Wild Cherry. Belkin also became involved in related rock 'n' roll business in 1976 when, on the strength of an unstoppable tune, he and record industry veteran Carl Maduri founded Sweet City, a label distributed by Epic Records. They immediately knocked it out of the park with Wild Cherry's "Play That Funky Music," the monster single from the pen of Wild Cherry founder Rob Parissi. Belkin continues to handle Parissi's royalty payments, which still come in healthily and regularly thanks to that singular track.

In a sense, "Play That Funky Music" represents Belkin's commercial high water mark. The single sold more than 2.5 million copies in the U.S. alone, hitting No. 1 on the Billboard Hot 100 charts in September 1976. The multi-platinum track continues to sell, and Vanilla Ice's version hit No. 4 in 1990. That unauthorized remake also won Parissi $500,000 in damages stemming from his copyright infringement suit against Ice.

Before Sweet City, however, there was Michael Stanley.

The Stanley Years

As the James Gang began to effectively run its course in the mid-'70s, Belkin's attention turned to Stanley, a man Belkin considers a family member. Before either man began his respective professional career in music, Belkin and Stanley each shared a love of baseball and great skill as pitchers. Each earned college scholarships for their athletic prowess, Belkin at Wisconsin, Stanley at Hiram College. Both love sports and both gave up the dream of a professional athletic career for music. And both are, in their distinctive ways, team players.

The Michael Stanley Band, circa 1980: bottom from left, Michael Stanley, Bob Pelander; center from left, Gary Markasky, Kevin Raleigh; top from left, Michael Gismondi, Tommy Dobeck.

LINER NOTES....................

Take it Easy, Desperado

Mike Belkin's respon- siveness and commitment helped get Glenn Frey out of a Columbus, Ohio, jail in 1974 after the former Eagles mainstay was busted for possession of pot following a show at Ohio State University's Mershon Auditorium that May 25.

Apparently, a Columbus cop walking by Frey's dressing room saw Frey toking up and arrested him. Frey, "may he rest in peace," reached out to Belkin, who was at home in Cleveland, and said he needed help. So Belkin called a Columbus attorney, who sprang Frey from the hoosegow after he spent one night.

Stanley, the one person other than a bank official who calls Mike Belkin by his birth name of Myron, is Belkin's go-to musician. Belkin is Stanley's trusted manager. These friends continue to come to each other's aid in times of need and join in celebration when times are good.

"There's a love affair between us," Belkin says. "As each day goes on, each week and month and year, it becomes a stronger bond." Loyalty is key.

Wildly popular in Cleveland, where he grew up and has always been based, Stanley has only occasionally been able to spread that status nationwide. Locally, however, it's a special story. It's been said that in Cleveland, Stanley was as popular as the Beatles.

Consider: August 10, 1984, was designated Michael Stanley Band Day in Cleveland, and in 1985, the Michael Stanley Band sold out a record-setting nine shows at the Front Row, a 3,200-seat theater in the round in Highland Heights that would close eight years later. At the Blossom Music Center, another prominent local venue, Stanley holds the attendance record—74,404—for a four-night stand in August 1982. In fact, it was during the last night of that fabled run that Belkin brought a horse onstage. The stunt provided further proof that rock 'n' roll and horses can make for an uncomfortable mix, as the entrance of a four-legged performer on stage is not among Stanley's fondest memories. At the same time, Belkin considers that Blossom stand his and Stanley's finest moment.

Making those performance records possible, Stanley crafted and performed such tunes as "Let's Get the Show on the Road," "My Town," "Rosewood Bitters," "Lover" and "Midwest Midnight," all Stanley classics that remain staples of his live shows. The Michael Stanley Band, which concertized from 1974 to 1987, became a household buzzword in Greater Cleveland. While Belkin was involved with Stanley very early in his career, he and Stanley would take their relationship to the next level. Belkin became Stanley's full-time manager toward the end of the 1970s, when MSB was well-established.

Stanley, Donnie Iris and Mark Avsec are the musicians with whom Belkin keeps in most regular contact because, like Belkin himself, they're still doing business. Jimmy Fox and Dale Peters, respectively drummer/founder and bassist of the James Gang, are effectively retired; the last time the definitive Gang, with guitarist Joe Walsh, toured was summer 2006.

After the Gang disbanded, Fox joined Belkin-Maduri Management and dealt with several of the musicians signed to Sweet City. Peters went into studio work, engineering and producing locally.

Iris and Avsec still work in Iris and the Cruisers, primarily in the Pittsburgh and Cleveland areas. Stanley, with his band the Resonators, regularly sells out his robust, entertaining shows. In keeping with

Michael Stanley at a pickup ball game with a band passing through Cleveland.

the Belkin proclivity for maintaining and extending relationships, the two bands also regularly share bills.

In addition, Stanley still turns out substantial, increasingly personal records mixed, as always, by Bill Szymczyk, his original patron, producer and longtime friend. (Szymczyk's other clients have included the Eagles, B.B. King—and the Walsh version of the James Gang.)

Bonding For Life

Bill Szymczyk and Mike Belkin have been constants in Michael Stanley's life for going on 50 years. Stanley met both in Cleveland in 1968, Szymczyk first.

It all began when Dick Korn, a bartender at Otto's Grotto in the old Statler Building downtown, invited his old friend Szymczyk to come to Cleveland to check out the rock scene. That introduction bore substantial creative and financial fruit. Over the course of six

Mike Belkin in the same pickup game.

months at the tail end of the 1960s, Szymczyk acquired the James Gang—and Silk, featuring someone named Michael Stanley Gee—for the ABC label.

That was a significant moment for the young bass player and songwriter. "It was a real label at that time, it was corporate, it was, like, wow, this is showbiz," Stanley recalls. "They gave us a $1,000 signing bonus, which we thought was amazing, and we went to New York to record ... and I'd never been to New York before. I felt like a farmer from Iowa, those big buildings and stuff."

Silk was the first band of any stature the Rocky River native had played in, and at the time, ABC was a strong label. But in the same amount of time that a rider can be bucked from a horse, circumstances can change. At the end of 1969, when Silk's "Smooth as Raw Silk" and the James Gang debut, "Yer' Album," were released,

ABC suddenly closed its New York office, morphing into Los Angeles-based ABC Dunhill.

Szymczyk went independent. Stanley left Silk. And Silk never made another album.

But Stanley certainly did. In fact, he produced 11 under the Michael Stanley Band name alone. As of February 2017, the total number of albums he has recorded was 34.

Becoming Michael Stanley

Cleveland's favorite rock 'n' roll son went by Michael Stanley Gee when Mike Belkin first managed him in Silk. But by 1973, he was Michael Stanley, still connected to Szymczyk but a few years away from his second, more lasting round with Belkin Personal Management.

After Szymczyk signed Silk to ABC and the Gang to ABC's short-lived subsidiary, Bluesway, Stanley went to the Belkin Productions office in Cleveland's near West Side. Decorated in what Stanley calls "cheap detective" style, the office was in a bank building catty corner to the original Belkin's Men's Shop.

The clothing store was still in business at that time, but Belkin Productions was consuming the time and attention of the Belkins. Growth was robust, partially due to the Belkin brothers' associate, Carl Maduri. Maduri would go on to launch Sweet City Records with Mike Belkin. The Belkins are acknowledged on the only Silk album, which features three songs written solely by Michael Stanley Gee and four he co-wrote. On the album, Silk management is credited to the "Wondrous Belkin Brothers of Cleveland."

When Belkin took over Silk's management, it began by booking the group into shows at high schools and local clubs such as the North Ridgeville Hullabaloo. Bigger gigs followed; Silk opened for Blood Sweat & Tears at the Syria Mosque in Pittsburgh on May 10, 1969, when BS&T was beginning an impressive run in the performing and recording industry. The very next night, Silk opened for Country Joe

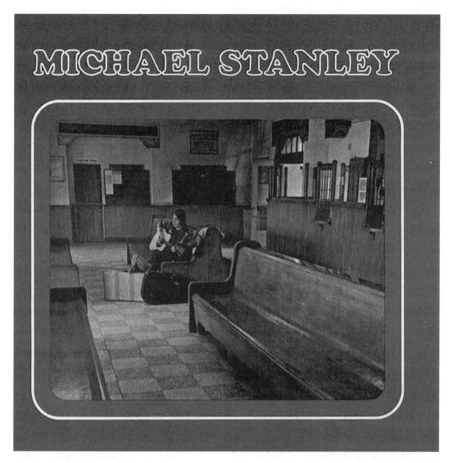

Michael Stanley's first solo album, for Tumbleweed.

and the Fish at Kent State University. It also did five Midwest dates with Sly and the Family Stone, then at the height of its popularity. The band was even due to open for Led Zeppelin at the old Musicarnival, but Stanley got sick that July 20 and the James Gang took Silk's place.

Silk and Led Zeppelin would eventually indirectly cross paths one other time. Zeppelin, of course, became a cornerstone of rock 'n' roll legend, Silk a footnote in Stanley's career. But it didn't start that way.

The Silk album came out in late October 1969, debuting in national rankings at No. 198, one spot ahead of "Led Zeppelin II," the album that starts with a little song called "Whole Lotta Love."

"The next week we were no longer on the charts at all and Led Zeppelin was No. 1. But for one week, we kicked those limeys' butts," jokes Stanley.

Stanley quit Silk shortly after, opting to stay home rather than join other band members who wanted to keep touring. Current events, especially the Vietnam War, loomed large in his decision.

Then a Hiram College student, Stanley figured if he quit school, he'd be prime draft fodder. So this star high-school pitcher, who entered Hiram on a baseball scholarship, hung in, graduating with a double major: comparative religions and sociology. He also got married his senior year and began to think about raising a family and settling down. He jokes that he still might open a sociology store.

As Stanley went domestic, Silk disbanded, Stanley drifted away from Belkin, and Szymczyk struck out on his own. But Szymczyk kept in touch, providing another connection that would prove to be instrumental for the future of both performers, music, and Belkin.

Rocky Mountain Way

As an independent producer, Szymczyk spent most of 1971 drumming up financing for Tumbleweed, a small independent label he launched with Denver entrepreneur Larry Ray, another ABC refugee.

The Colorado capital was becoming a magnet for rock and rollers, drawing hippies like James Gang guitar icon Joe Walsh and a favorite of his, Dan Fogelberg, as well as Buffalo Springfield alumni Stephen Stills and Richie Furay. And thanks to Szymczyk, Michael Stanley, who finally dropped the "Gee" in the Rockies.

"Szymczyk called me out of the blue, he said, are you still writing songs? Yeah, I'm writing a bunch of songs. He said, you want to make a record?" Stanley recalls. Are you kidding? Despite his youthful ambivalence about being a band leader, Stanley likes to make records. His first one would turn out to be a honey.

Not only does his eponymous debut have beautiful songs like "Rosewood Bitters" and "Denver Rain," it features a cover of Bob

Michael Stanley's second album, on MCA, affirmed his reputation
as a singer-songwriter.

Dylan's "Subterranean Homesick Blues," along with heavyweight help from Walsh, fellow guitar hotshot Rick Derringer, and Todd Rundgren on clavinette. But the album is not attributed to Michael Gee— Michael Stanley's name at the time— because, by the freakiest of coincidences, a Canadian named Arthur Gee was already signed to the Tumbleweed label.

"We can't have two guys on a seven-man roster named Gee," Szymczyk told Stanley. "You have to change your name." Szymczyk said there was no time to think about it, there was a record to release.

"Szymczyk said, what's your middle name?" Stanley told him. "He said that's cool, that won't offend anybody. So I became Michael Stanley."

The record received good reviews, Stanley says, but Tumbleweed folded in 1973 after Gulf & Western turned off the financial spigot. As an example of transactions that are largely out of the artist's control, Stanley's contract was sold to MCA.

That same year, with Szymczyk again producing, Stanley recorded "Friends & Legends," even as Stanley worked in Cleveland as regional manager of Disc Records, a six-state, 20-store chain. In a unique intermingling of his life at the time, Stanley would lay down tracks while on vacation; "Friends & Legends" was largely recorded in the Rockies. Michael Stanley the performer would then return to Cleveland where as regional manager, he'd order the finished album for his stores. Helping along that sweet loop was his connection to David Spero, a music business kid who, like Stanley's father, Stan, worked for Malrite Communications. Malrite was a significant radio industry player that owned such stations as AMer WHK, where Stanley's father, Stan Gee, was a salesman, and WMMS, the FM power where Spero was a DJ.

According to Mike Olszewski's "Radio Daze," Walsh alerted Spero to Stanley's talent. Then Stanley's father gave Spero Stanley's Tumbleweed record and *voila*—Stanley was on the radio. While serendipitous relationships certainly streamlined Stanley's path to initial exposure over the airwaves, his longer-term success would be decided by discerning radio and concert audiences. Meanwhile, his commercial success would be influenced by his management. Spero left WMMS in 1974 to manage Stanley until 1977, when Belkin took over.

Finding the Right Fit

In the early '70s, with two albums under his belt, Stanley had to choose between remaining an employee in the retail record business and leading a band. Stability versus uncertainty; it wasn't an easy choice.

MSB in 1977, from a photo by Bob Ferrell in Scene Magazine's 10th Anniversary is-sue, published July 17, 1980. At top, Bob Pelander, bottom from left: Tommy Dobeck, Michael Stanley, Jonah Koslen, and Michael Gismondi.

So early on, he choose to keep one foot in both worlds and didn't tour or form a band. That choice likely impeded his success in the short term, he says. His decision made sense, though—Stanley's wife quit her job, gave birth to twins, and the couple bought a new car.

While trying to balance income and exposure, Michael Stanley the artist promoted his own record at a store that wasn't part of the record chain that employed Michael Stanley, regional record store manager. Stanley's boss was not conflicted when he discovered the promotion; he fired him just two weeks after the Stanleys' twins were born. While it was a blow at the time, in retrospect, losing his Disc Records position seems trivial, especially considering his increased airplay and growing reputation. It might be said that circumstances forced Stanley to stop straddling and instead, saddle up.

He would commit to a full-time career as an artist, and what a successful career it would turn out to be. It began with those durable solo records, continuing with notching hits with the Michael Stanley Band, recording for three major labels and performing pretty much at the frequency and venue of his choice.

"We did it and some of us are still doing it," says Stanley. "MSB lasted 13 years and put out 11 albums; who else do you know who put out 11 albums?"

Before he could accomplish those feats, however, Stanley had to make another big transition. This one would require him to grow from singer-songwriter and solo artist to eventually become a band leader. And while Stanley may have been ambivalent about being a front man, he has never shrunk from a challenge.

So in 1973, he launched MSB featuring singer-songwriter Jonah Koslen, bassist Danny Pecchio and drummer Tommy Dobeck. Pecchio came from Glass Harp and Dobeck came from Circus, a power-pop band with a rabid Cleveland following that made a single album for Metromedia. Koslen would go on to form Breathless, another band Belkin managed.

Again, Szymczyk was instrumental to Stanley in the process, leveraging industry connections to land Stanley on Epic, the first major label for which MSB recorded. Szymczyk connected Stanley to Steve Popovich, then vice president of artists & repertoire at Epic. Among Popovich's more prominent signings: Cheap Trick, MSB, Boston, Ted Nugent—and through Sweet City, Wild Cherry.

"When I got involved with the Michael Stanley Band, Jonah (Koslen) was already the lead singer," Belkin says. "I think David (Spero) was with them for a while. But Michael felt it was time for him to change course. He felt that David had gotten him and the band as far as David could take him."

Belkin notes that while he prefers to steer clear of musical decisions, for MSB at that moment, he encouraged a significant change. Belkin told Stanley that he, not Koslen, had to be the magnet, the focus, of MSB.

"Jonah was the lead singer and he was up front, but everybody knew it as the Michael Stanley Band, so I said to Michael, OK, look, you've got to step out," Belkin says. " '*You* are the Michael Stanley Band, not Jonah Koslen.' He was comfortable doing what he was doing, but once I was able to convince him to be the upfront guy and the lead singer, the whole band changed.

"I didn't think there was enough interaction with the audience," Belkin says. "Michael was very hot in the '80s. Women used to rush the stage—guys, too, but mostly women—and as opposed to kicking them off, I had told security, do not make them get off the stage." That approach would result in a balancing act for the security in managing the safety of the band and the fans while helping encourage enthusiasm for the group.

Belkin doesn't think that new emphasis caused a personal conflict between Stanley and Koslen. Perhaps that's due to a surge in popularity that was good for everyone connected to MSB and to Stanley, both as performer and on the personal level.

Stanley is always generous with sharing credit and the spotlight. Stanley encouraged keyboardist Kevin Raleigh as lead singer on Raleigh's tune, "He Can't Love You," MSB's biggest hit.

"I never set out to be the guy in front," he says. Mostly, the decision seems to have been driven by Belkin's counsel that's confirmed by Stanley's sense of the audience that the band attracted. "If you travel around the country, anywhere they'll go, I remember that record, and then they'll go, who was that? We were pretty faceless, we were the guys next door. But then again so many of those bands were, like REO (Speedwagon) and Styx and Kansas."

Belkin's innate showman sense however, told him that Stanley had to be front and center. "People started enjoying Michael up there as the lead singer," Belkin says. "But Michael didn't just cut Jonah out of everything. Jonah still sang, as a backup singer, but he wasn't the guy up front with the microphone. And it had to be that way. It just made sense. People knew Michael sang the songs; it was right on the CD. Now they were able to see the guy they heard. Until then, he was background vocals and he played guitar."

Choppy Waters

Epic put MSB on tour with teen idol Rex Smith, who hit with "You Take My Breath Away," behind MSB's first album, "You Break It... You Bought It." In a rather unusual contractual arrangement, the two groups alternated as opening act and headliner. Epic underwrote the tour but charged expenses against record sales, trapping the band in the hole that had been dug for them. "Everything a record company 'gives' to a band monetarily is recoupable for them. Money is charged against royalties that the record company pays the artist—that is, if there's anything left to pay after expenses," says Belkin.

A recording deal includes the costs of studio time, paying musicians and the producer, mastering the album, and all expenses. All these are recoupable costs for the label. So, too, are the costs of pressing the album, cover artwork, advertising and promotion, and advance money for touring including vehicles, food and lodging.

Say an album costs $100,000 to produce and the band needs a place to stay and money for "incidental" expenses like food. The band has to pay all that back before it can turn a profit. The arrangement sets the bar extraordinarily high. The band must sell a huge number of records just to break even, let alone begin earning royalties above and beyond the recoupable expenses.

"You get an advance of, say, $100,000. They don't give it to you all at once," Belkin says. "So it's important to watch your expenses so at the end of the day you have something left over. So you get a statement and all these expenses are deducted, so you end up not even close to netting $100,000. Until all the expenses are recouped you don't find a big check."

Each deal is essentially for one album, and the budget goes up on each subsequent recording. "That's why they can say the Michael Stanley Band just signed a $5 million contract with Epic Records," says Stanley, but that's true only if a contract goes to term, like 12 years. The label can cancel the contract anytime a band fails to sell a predetermined amount of records.

"That being said, Sweet City Records worked the same way," says Belkin, who struck gold many times over with the custom label he founded with Carl Maduri. "That's the way the record companies work." The difference with Sweet City was one tune, Wild Cherry's blockbuster "Play That Funky Music."

Stanley's success was less mercurial but longer-lasting. The follow-up to "You Break It … " was "Ladies' Choice," and then came the double album, "Stagepass." That Epic swansong, recorded at Henry LoConti's Agora and a favorite of Stanley fans, sold around a half-million copies while the first two had sold about 100,000 each, Stanley says. Despite that success, it was time to leave Epic. "I think at that point, whatever the next level of the contract was, they were going to have to make a major investment, really up their ante," Stanley says. "It was, like, we like them, but do we like them that much?"

Stanley speaks as if he's inside the head of an Epic executive circa 1977: "What's the upside of these guys for a fourth album versus taking a crapshoot on six new bands for the same amount of money? And much like professional athletic teams, if somebody was your champion at the record company, if they leave, you have no champion anymore." For MSB, that champion was Steve Popovich, who in fact would leave Epic that very year to found Cleveland International, where he struck gold—again, many times, despite his own longstanding dispute with Epic—by signing Meat Loaf.

With the ascendancy of Michael Stanley and the formation of Sweet City—not to mention the establishment of a custom O'Jays label—Cleveland was gaining notice as a rock 'n' roll hotbed. Stanley and Belkin were eager to lead the charge, too, though Stanley seemed to be stranded again, this time in the middle of the commercial road.

Chapter 7

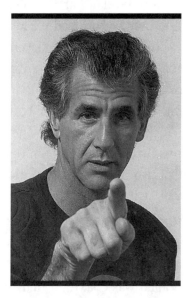

In the Thick of It

Tonight I'm gonna try a little harder
But come the light I'm gonna be working
Working again...

Michael Stanley Band ~ *Working Again*

As the 1970s were, shall we say, maturing, so too, was the Belkins' business as revenue grew and the pace picked up. Not only was Mike Belkin managing the Michael Stanley Band, Sweet City was on a roll and Belkin Productions was rocking. Rocking not just because of the legendary World Series of Rock, a multi-act stadium extravaganza that ran from 1974 to 1980. There also were numerous regular concerts.

In 1976 alone, the Belkins produced shows all over the Midwest, at least half of them in the Cleveland area. These included individual shows and entire tours, many produced exclusively by Belkin Productions and others as co-productions. Artists included: Cat Stevens, dates by Sweet, Ted Nugent, Bette Midler, the Who, David Bowie, Joni Mitchell, Queen, Grover Washington, Kiss, Black Oak Arkansas, the Tubes, Peter Frampton, Uriah Heep, Robin Trower, Lynyrd Skynyrd, Johnny Winter, Joe Cocker, and Genesis. The Belkins' geographic range spanned their own back yard (Patti Smith at the Allen Theatre) to Charleston, South Carolina (a co-promotion with country and western legend Conway Twitty).

"We were doing stuff all the time," says Belkin. "The '70s were extremely busy. Jules was on the road far more than me; I was managing bands in Cleveland and working more of the Cleveland dates."

What that also entailed was coaxing Michael Stanley toward star status and pushing Sweet City as far as possible. The trajectories of each were different though the timing overlapped. Stanley became a unique local phenomenon while Wild Cherry, Sweet City's premier act, went worldwide—on vinyl and cassette, if not on the road.

The year both hit was 1976. Stanley and Wild Cherry toured with various artists connected to Epic Records, the label that distributed both Michael Stanley Band and Wild Cherry albums. But by 1977, Stanley had hired Belkin as his manager and was ready to leave Epic.

Starting with the James Gang and Joe Walsh lawsuits, litigation became a frequent theme for Belkin and the groups he managed. Nevertheless, the courtroom drama didn't sever the connections Belkin forged with those bands. In fact, Belkin's acumen with royalty and contractual matters made many acts more likely to seek Belkin out as a manager.

During that key search for a label suited to MSB, the bond between Stanley and Belkin deepened. The three-year management deal the two signed in October 1977 gave Belkin 20 percent of Stanley's

Left to right, Michael Stanley, Barry Gabel and Mike Belkin at a 1986 Michael Stanley concert celebrating the decision to build the Rock and Roll Hall of Fame and Museum on Cleveland's lakefront. Mike Belkin was part of the corporate committee that helped bring this landmark institution to Cleveland.

earnings, unless an independent booking agent was involved; then the split was 15 percent for Belkin and 10 percent for the outside agent. After a few more signed renewals, the arrangement evolved into a handshake deal that could only be breached by death.

"For me, you trust someone until they give you a reason not to, and I still trust Mike," Stanley says.

"Forty-plus years ago, when I started to manage Michael's music career, I did not really know about him as a person," says Belkin. "It didn't take very long for me to know that he was the type of individual that I wanted to be associated with. I would do whatever it took for me to help him be a successful rock 'n' roll star."

What Belkin did primarily was get Stanley better pay for his increasingly popular gigs. And in conversations with impresarios outside the local market, Belkin would point to MSB's increasing draw, suggesting a date that paid $5,000 before now demanded $7,500. In Cleveland, Belkin says, "knowing I wanted to build the market for him, I would get him as much money as I felt he deserved."

On the label front, where Szymczyk arranged the Epic deal, Belkin arranged signings with Arista Records and EMI America, Stanley's last major label.

Each deal began promisingly, though Stanley came to view the record industry with disdain. "It was a whore's business," he says. "Management is the one that you get to fight the battles. That's how they earn their percentage. It's like when Allen Klein took over the Stones and the Beatles, he got some of their publishing back."

On his first two albums, Stanley retained only a "very small portion" of the publishing rights to the semi-hits "Rosewood Bitters" and "Let's Get the Show on the Road." Since Belkin took over his management, however, Stanley has owned his tunes. As his manager, Belkin gets a cut to handle the publishing, copyrighting and accounting—and to be a staunch, informed advocate for MSB.

Cleveland Rocks

In the late 1970s, the city of Cleveland was in disarray. Population was bleeding out of a proud city that 50 years earlier had been the country's fifth largest metropolis. Manufacturing jobs left town for more receptive climates, a public school system that was once a model for the nation was crumbling and city politics were a testament to corruption and cronyism.

But against that sobering background, it was also a great time for music in Cleveland, due to what Stanley calls the triumvirate: FM station WMMS, *Scene* magazine, and Belkin Productions—Mike and Jules Belkin's booming business. There was also the Agora, a proving ground for artists. Henry LoConti's club, first on East 24th Street and

In 1985, Belkin Productions moved into this building in downtown Chagrin Falls, Ohio, southeast of Cleveland and close to Mike Belkin's rural home.

later on Euclid Avenue at East 55th, featured acts that would go on to larger, Belkin-booked venues. The Agora also was known for the 'MMS-sponsored Coffee Break concerts. Jane Scott, the rock 'n' roll writer at the *Plain Dealer*, was a big MSB supporter. So was Bruno Bornino at the old *Cleveland Press*. The crowds kept growing, and MSB even did well in places like St. Louis, southern Florida and Texas. But its stronghold was Ohio, and in Cleveland, you couldn't miss MSB. In fact, you couldn't escape it.

WMMS trend setter Kid Leo would play one side of an MSB album, then interview Stanley. Then he'd play the other side—and interview Stanley again. "You couldn't turn on the radio without being subjected to us one way or another," Stanley says. "We couldn't get arrested in L.A. Did great in San Francisco. When we were selling 90,000 seats up here, we were lucky to sell 3,000 in Columbus.

"Everybody realized that one hand was washing the other and anybody who could help anybody else would," Stanley recalls. "If Belkin was breaking a band, with the support of 'MMS that band would benefit both of them and *Scene* magazine would have a lot of stuff to write about. *Scene* was the internet back then; if you wanted to know what was going on, you read *Scene*."

MSB was battle-tested and eager to use Cleveland as a launch pad for a national campaign. "When I signed with Mike again as the Michael Stanley Band, a lot of the groundwork had already been done. He wasn't signing a fledgling, unknown out-of-the box band," Stanley says, noting MSB had been touring for four years and had three nationally distributed albums under its belt. "The question was, how do we roll to the next level? Mike and his organization would be the one to do that."

In terms of sales, MSB posted national numbers, but "you wanted to pick up the level with each album ... more sales, more tour gigs, more radio play, whatever you do it would be more. That's just the way the business was and probably still is."

In 1979, MSB began staging multiple-night stands at a single venue, a sign the band was big-time, at least in Cleveland. The turning point was that November 21-25, consecutive Thanksgiving weekend gig at Cleveland's Palace Theatre. The run was MSB's first in the old vaudeville venue.

One of those five nights was a "black tie" show, also known as "tux night." That event was Belkin's idea. "Did I instigate it?" this lover of all things theatrical is asked. "You show up at the theater in a pair of jeans, you can't come in," he recalls. "It was a five-day thing and to make the days special, I made one night of that run black tie only."

"Mike comes from the old school," says Stanley. "It's Mike's kind of thing: Let's do something bizarre. Kind of like old show biz." At that Palace run, he notes, "our opening act was a guy who walked on swords."

Gary Markasky, left, and Michael Stanley at the storied "tuxedo show" of 1979.

This was rock 'n' roll, where spectacle matters. Belkin likes spectacle, and nobody does it better.

Fast-forward to New Year's Eve 1981, when Belkin persuaded Stanley (and Coliseum ownership, and also liability management

The July 19-25, 1979 cover of Scene Magazine *promotes a Michael Stanley Band show at the Coliseum and the latest album, "Greatest Hints," with MSB Week. Mark Holan's cover story asks, "Will America get the hint now?"*

companies) to allow MSB guitarist Gary Markasky to enter the old Richfield Coliseum in a highly spectacular fashion.

During the entrance, Markasky played guitar, while descending from the rafters on a cable, illuminated by a spotlight—and wearing only a diaper. As you might imagine, the rockin' New Year's baby wowed the 21,000 fans. It was a gag, of course, but it served its purpose well as anyone who was lucky enough to be there told all their friends, who told others. It was leveraging an age-old form of social media—word-of-mouth—over 20 years before Facebook.

Not all of Belkin's creative jokester energy was directed at creating a better, more memorable show. Belkin is also quite a joker off stage, often pulling pranks just because he can. Stanley recalls a late night incident with the full MSB entourage at a pricey New York steakhouse after one performance by the band in the city.

Encouraged by Belkin, the party kept ordering expensive bottles of wine and top-cut steaks. At the finale of this indulgence, Belkin excused himself to supposedly take a phone call—and didn't return, sending Stanley and his road manager into a panic, Belkin says, chuckling.

Stanley asked road manager Jim Soffos how much cash he had on him. Soffos said about $200. Stanley had about $600. The bill was around $1,600. What was a rock 'n' roll band to do? Stanley looked to the edge of the room and saw Belkin chatting with the maître d'. Belkin was cracking up. "I left. I paid the bill. They didn't know that," Belkin says. "He'll put you on as far as he can," Stanley says of his manager. "To watch 15 people squirm out there, that's the highlight of his month."

But of course, most of the music business is not constructed around gags and giggles. When he signed a contract to a major label the first time around with Silk, Stanley enjoyed the rush as a record business baby. But by 1976, when he signed with Epic, he was an adult and the bloom was beginning to come off the rose. It was time to get serious.

Advance to the Rear

On the label front, MSB was a known quantity by now, so a Belkin meeting with Clive Davis was not a stretch. Besides, he knew the legendary music influence from Columbia Records, where Davis was president from 1967 to 1973.

In 1974, Davis founded Arista Records. MSB is the only band that Belkin successfully pitched to Davis as MSB signed a contract and recorded two albums for Arista. "Cabin Fever" came out in 1978 and "Greatest Hints" broke in 1979 in a far chillier atmosphere.

Initially, Arista put muscle behind MSB, sending the band to Wales to record "Cabin Fever" with producer Robert John Lange, a master board man who would later produce AC/DC, Def Leppard—and his then-wife, country megastar Shania Twain. "Why Should Love Be This Way," a ballad from "Fever," even hit the national charts. The group ran into trouble with "Hints," however. And while Belkin, ever the diplomat, speaks kindly of Davis, it seems clear that Davis didn't treat MSB very well.

According to Stanley, Davis "decided he wanted to be heavily involved in picking out the tunes" for "Hints," so MSB recorded the album with Harry Maslin, Davis' hand-picked producer. Maslin had just come off helming "Fame," David Bowie's first U.S. No. 1 single.

"We gave him, like, 20 songs, and he picked the nine or 10 he wanted on the record. He was the boss, and you're going on the assumption that, hey, if these are the songs he wants, he's going to be behind them," says Stanley. But that was not the case. When Davis heard what MSB had recorded for "Hints," he said, "I'm not into this," Stanley recalls.

"He went as far as to say, I'm not even going to release it. To which me and Mike said, we gotta work, this is going to affect us being able to tour. All right, (Davis said), I'm going to release it but I'm not going to do anything for it, which in the record business is the kiss of death. It was the first time I'd come up against that blatant of an approach.

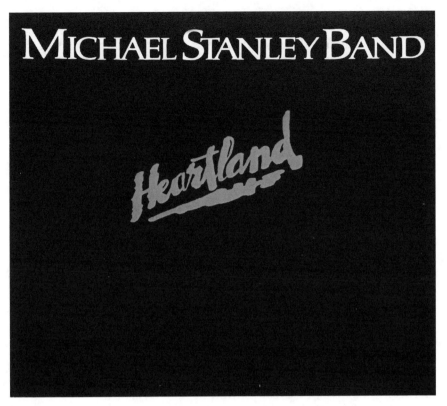

MSB's first EMI album.

It was done in person and it was all very matter of fact; there was no trying to finesse it."

"I liked Clive a lot," maintains Belkin. "We got along real well. Clive has supposedly a golden ear, and you can't tell that person, Oh, you should like that. Clive was known to have good ears, and he had a good taste for music and had a lot of success at Columbia prior to Arista."

Davis's stance effectively killed the deal with Arista. "The album dies, and that's the end," says Belkin. "We did our two albums and he didn't want to renew."

Taking Matters Into Their Own Hands

After the deal with Arista collapsed, "we were without a label but we were obviously still growing, which was weird, kind of freewheeling around the harbor," says Stanley. "Mike's job at that point was the most important: get us another label—and we were having a hard time getting a label."

Gloom set in. Had MSB come to the end of the line, even though they had cached a bunch of good songs, ready to record? Trouble was, MSB had no entrée to a studio—and worse, no money to hold them over.

Time for self-determination, and Belkin played a key role. He arranged for MSB to record its new album locally. MSB would produce and pay for the recording itself and, if no major label grabbed it, would release it independently.

"Mike got us a great deal at a brand-new studio in town, Beachwood Studios," Stanley says. "The deal was we would kind of dry-run the studio and let them find out where all the kinks were and in exchange they'd give us a great minimum rate to record."

The first band to record at Beachwood, MSB would work all night and leave before the studio's daytime business. The result of that innovative approach was "Heartland," the first of four albums for EMI. After "Heartland," securing an EMI contract would be relatively easy.

The songs were essentially ready to record, and it was Belkin's job to shop the album around once it was done. For the first time, MSB was the object of a bidding war because Belkin had a finished, professionally produced record for sale. The deal with EMI was good, the budget was good, "and the best thing about it is when a label signs a band, a lot of the people at the label get excited," Stanley says. With the record all but finished, all that was left was cosmetics, like the cover. The album was fast-tracked and out within three weeks.

"We started running and nobody stopped us and nobody stopped them," Stanley says of EMI. "And there was synergy: Around that

Mike Belkin and Michael Stanley are always willing to support good causes, as with this show in 1985.

time, MTV started, and MTV was hungry for content. They didn't even care what it was. They made somebody else pay for the video, they just gave it to them and they ran it and they made all their money and they hadn't laid out any upfront money."

MSB generated three videos from the EMI albums it released between 1980 and 1983. The key record was "Heartland," with "He Can't Love You," its first single, sparked by a solo from Clarence Clemons, the tenor sax player in Bruce Springsteen's band. "Lover," too, was a potent "Heartland" track.

Released in 1980, "Heartland" topped out at No. 86 on the *Billboard* charts. "He Can't Love You," written and sung by keyboardist Kevin Raleigh, reached No. 33 on the singles charts, and "Lover," which Stanley wrote and sang, reached No. 68. Success and stability seemed within Stanley's grasp.

Moving up, Taking Their Lumps

"Heartland" stayed on the charts for a year and a half. There were tours with Mahogany Rush, John Cougar Mellencamp, Eddie Money, Cheap Trick. "We were never off the road," says Stanley. "For the first time, we had a record company that was going, hey, we need another album right away."

The band tried to keep momentum going by writing on the road, at the same time earning its stripes onstage. "It was great. It's what you thought it was supposed to be," Stanley says of that period. "We were a good live band; I think we always got more fans through our live act than our albums."

Belkin did what a manager should, dealing with promoters and booking agents, trying to slot back-to-back dates to minimize travel and expenses. He also massaged the truth when necessary, perhaps playing a role in a particularly problematic tour as opening act for Jeff Beck.

The tour with guitarist Beck attests to Belkin's managerial creativity and guile. Beck was in his fusion phase, while MSB was a six- to seven-piece mainstream rock band with four-part harmonies.

"We started in Florida, and every gig we went north got worse and worse. People hated us; we'd never run into that before, because we were standing between them and Jeff Beck; it wasn't a good match,"

belkin productions & wmms INVITE YOU TO
THE ANNUAL HOLIDAY BASH

Michael Stanley Band

the front row

SIX INCREDIBLE NIGHTS!
DEC. 18, 20, 21, 23, 26 & 28 8 P.M.

UP CLOSE
IN THE ROUND

Reserved Tickets: $14.75
ON SALE SATURDAY (Nov. 16)
at the Front Row Box Office &
all Ticketron Locations
CHARGE BY PHONE:
Cleveland 524-0000
Elsewhere in Ohio
1-800-362-0400

This 1985 ad attests to MSB's multi-night might.

Stanley says. "When we went out with the Doobie Brothers, Foreigner, or Styx, it was all a good match." Beck fans were there to hear their guitar hero. MSB felt worse than unwelcome.

Playing its set felt "like we were stealing time and money from them," but Beck wouldn't come on stage any sooner. So it was the audience that was closed; it could go with the flow, it could opt out or it could attack. When it came to MSB, it attacked. MSB fought back in a unique fashion—until it finally couldn't stand it.

"The last show we did, we kind of got into the stubborn mode of we're not going to give up. It was like, Oh, yeah, we're going to turn it up louder and play faster. The last show we did we took every song in the set and we ran them all together so there'd be no dead air for them to boo," Stanley says. The attitude was, "'It doesn't matter. Somebody just keep playing. They can only boo once; the end.'"

After that gig on October 7, 1980, at the Capitol Theatre in Passaic, N.J., MSB was supposed to go to New York City. No way. "I called Mike and said, we can't do this. We go to New York, every reviewer in the world's going to be there and we're going to come off terrible," says Stanley, who was struggling to preserve his group's reputation as well as its morale. He told Belkin the crowd would savage MSB and he had to get the band off the date "so it doesn't tarnish our reputations. He did it, he came up with this whole big medical back story where the bass player had to be taken to urgent care.

"Mike was usually the sharpest guy in the room," says Stanley. "He had his facts down, he knew what he was talking about, and if he found himself in a position where he didn't want to be, he could bullshit his way through with the best of them. That's a wonderful attribute in a manager. He would convince me (about something), and then, when we were alone, I'd say, when did that happen? He'd say it didn't happen. He kept the wolves at bay.

"He's there to cover your ass and managers are there to do whatever they can for you and to be your shield. They're there to be the bad guy." And that was a role Belkin was willing to play, if necessary.

Cleveland Calling

It was 1983, the year of "You Can't Fight Fashion," the band's last recording for EMI America. "Fashion" featured two tracks that smacked of hit: "Someone Like You" and "My Town." After the success of "Someone Like You," EMI called on Stanley, pressuring him for an even stronger follow-up.

"They came to me and said, we got to have a single and we want an anthem," he says. "An anthem's really got to touch just about everybody. What does everybody relate to? Your town, wherever you live, your city, your home, so that's where that came from," says this

From Scene, *1986.*

Michael Stanley and his young friend, Sam Belkin.

adaptable pro. "It's only a Cleveland song when I sing it, and there's nothing in the song that says anything about Cleveland." Stanley kept the tune generic on purpose and on order. It's a song built to be zoned.

"My Town" began to take off. "Then the record company got this idea, because it started to happen real quickly, everywhere, so (keyboardist) Bob Pelander and I went to New York and we overdubbed about 100 different versions of the song so somewhere in the song we yelled out a city name," Stanley says. "There's a thing right before the line, 'This is my town,' where you would yell Oklahoma City, Dallas, Portland. There are actually people out there who think the song is about their city because that's the only version they ever heard." It was musical mass customization—and it was brilliant.

Ironically, "My Town" would also be Stanley's last brush with national fame. Even as the song was ascending, EMI choked it. Neither

Stanley nor Belkin can explain why. Talk about a year of highs and lows and you're talking about 1983 if you're Michael Stanley and Mike Belkin.

What Falls Away, What Lasts

When EMI approached Stanley and Belkin seeking a six-month extension on its soon-to-expire contract, Stanley balked. "My Town" was "screaming up the charts," the album was doing the same, "and for the first time in my career I thought I was in a position of some kind of power," Stanley says. He and Belkin talked it over and decided to call EMI's bluff.

Stanley told Belkin he thought this was "the first time we've had any power. I think we should exercise it: sign us now—the single's already up to No. 50 in two weeks, the album's up to No. 50, we were on tour. Long story short, I said no, we're not going to sign the extension," Stanley recalls of a tense conversation with EMI executives. "We'll play out the contract, and if you want us you can sign us again. And to my total shock, they said, Oh, yeah? And they pulled out all support from the single and the album—everything."

"I had discussed it with them," Belkin recalls of EMI, but he ultimately left the decision up to Stanley. "It's his life, his career, and he's a great guy and I respect him," he says. "It was an important decision. It's history.

"This was a career decision—not my career, his career," Belkin says. "I respect him, he respects me. We have a lot of history behind us, and ultimately, we've had a lot of history since that." Still, the EMI rejection rankles both men.

"It was a crusher," Stanley says. "Everybody felt mad, me more than anybody else because I made the decision. And it affected a lot of people." Despite this setback, the relationship with Belkin perseveres.

"If he had been adamantly against it, I probably would have gone with what he said. We knew there was a chance this could backfire, but we really thought the odds were in our favor because of what

Left to right, Mike Belkin, photographer Janet Macoska, Michael Stanley and Barry Gabel at a 2015 release party for Stanley's CD "And Then..." at the Rock and Roll Hall of Fame.

the record was doing. Why would they want to throw that away?" Stanley says.

"The record company didn't really go after the song like they should have, really get behind Michael like they should have," says Belkin, but speculating on what might have happened had EMI committed more deeply is fruitless.

"It was like a one-sided deal: Do this and we'll work that, give us a six-month extension and we'll work the single. Or else we're going to drop it." Something went sour and Belkin isn't sure what. "It was like blackmail."

Michael Stanley's Second Act

After the EMI deal went south, MSB hung on. Even without an album to promote, it sold gangbusters in Cleveland, drawing large crowds until it finally called it a day in 1987.

"Mike's taken a lot of shit over the years from people, fans especially, that he's the reason we weren't superstars," Stanley says. "And nothing could be further from the truth. Did he make mistakes along the way? I'm sure he did. I can't give you specifics. Could he have done something better? Probably. It's like, couldn't you have written better songs? When we got to the point where we sold out four nights in Blossom, and we were the biggest thing that had

Michael Stanley, left, with Mike Belkin, when the Belkin brothers were honored with the prestigious Martha Joseph Prize at the 2015 Cleveland Arts Prize awards ceremony.

ever come out of Cleveland, at that point in time I owed Mike about $300,000 to $400,000 he had fronted us to keep us going—band bills and salaries; we were on the debit side. Even though we were playing constantly, most of it was (as an) opening (act); there were five or six cities around the country where we could headline."

MSB was God in Cleveland, however, Stanley says, noting that even the Rolling Stones are a local band somewhere. "When we sold out those four nights at Blossom, I was finally able to pay Mike back all the money, and that's what people don't realize; we would have never gotten to that point had he not supported us financially as well as emotionally. Mike Belkin believed in us and backed it up.

"It's that old 'put your money where your mouth is,'" Stanley says, speaking of Belkin. "He did."

Nevertheless, the band's fortunes took a turn for the worse, precipitated by the collapse of the EMI arrangement. In 1986, MSB bookings dropped dramatically, according to show logs Belkin keeps. That also was the year that MSB released its final album, "Inside Moves." After the breakup of MSB in 1987, Stanley went out on his own, both as a solo act and as leader of bands including the Ghost Poets and the Resonators.

"It's the American thing," says Stanley. "Nobody knows who finishes in second place. It's first or nothing. There's no gradation. I am quite comfortable with the term 'journeyman.' " And whenever Stanley has reassembled and diversified, Belkin has been there, still scheming, still taking care of his friend.

One of Belkin's latest Stanley brand extensions is a VLT, or video lottery terminal, at the Hard Rock Casino, a 2,000-seat venue in Northfield, Ohio that Stanley regularly sells out. These sophisticated slot machines feature Stanley's name and image, joining another local hero, Bernie Kosar—and pop stars Britney Spears and Ellen DeGeneres. Stanley gets a cut of the play, Belkin a much smaller cut. "It's found money," says Belkin. "He doesn't have to do anything." So the Michael Stanley slot machines are as close to a sure thing as possible.

Life, both business and personal, presents us with risks, its gambles and outcomes determined by chance, as Belkin learned as a child. And Belkin and Stanley would probably agree that business decisions, no matter how informed, are ultimately gambles as well. In the music business in the 1970s and 1980s, creating and managing your own recording label represented a big opportunity—and required a major leap of faith.

Chapter 8

Motown on the Cuyahoga

How can you sit still when music's hot?

Q ~ *Dancin' Man*

In the mid-1970s, Michael Stanley was on the rise, Belkin Productions was booming, and rock 'n' roll was big business, particularly in Cleveland. The World Series of Rock was setting attendance records, *Scene* was the tribal drum for area rock 'n' rollers, WMMS was the go-to radio station, and Belkin Productions was producing shows all over the region. Entertainment entrepreneurialism and creative collaboration provided a cyclical undercurrent that fueled the music scene, including album sales. According to the Recording

Industry Association of America, total sales of albums (records and tapes) hit $2.36 billion in 1975, and $2.74 billion—then an all-time high—the following year. In 1976, the record industry also instituted the platinum designation, signifying sales of more than two million singles and/or one million albums.

Album sales were hot. No wonder Mike Belkin was interested in launching a record label, and he was right on time. In 1976, as Stanley was looking for a new label, Belkin and longtime record company insider Carl Maduri persuaded Epic Records to promote and distribute Sweet City Records, a custom imprint based in Cleveland. Epic signed onto this arrangement because of "Play That Funky Music," a tune written by Rob Parissi and performed by his group, Wild Cherry.

That single effectively captured the pop zeitgeist of the day, laying Parissi's catchy lyric over a tough guitar-and-drums track that vamped

on "Fire," a No. 1 hit for the Ohio Players in early 1975. Fifteen years later, "Play That Funky Music" enjoyed a second chart life when an unauthorized take not only sold well, it also netted Parissi and Belkin-Maduri big money in copyright infringement damages.

Sweet City Records strutted out of the gates with a swagger. "When 'Play That Funky Music' hit, it was an instant smash and we were asked to form our own record company, Sweet City Records, by Epic, because they thought we were extremely creative, we had this crap that came out and was a monster, so they wanted to lock us into a deal," Belkin says. "Carl was able to go out and find some talent he thought would be good for the record company and sell some records."

Not only was the time right for Belkin to launch an album, the moment was at hand for Cleveland itself to make a soulful stand.

Wild Cherry, from left: Allen Wentz, Ron Beitle, Bryan Bassett, Rob Parissi, Coogie Stoddart, and Mark Avsec.

"Detroit had Motown. Philadelphia has Philadelphia International. Chicago has Mercury," *Plain Dealer* rock scribe Jane Scott wrote on March 26, 1976. "How can Cleveland be big time without its own record label?" many musicians have asked.

"Cleveland now has one. It's called Sweet City. And it's a first."

Maduri's expertise was music while Belkin's was promotion, making for a partnership that seemed natural. The duo first heard Wild Cherry at Cleveland Recording, where the band was laying down tracks that studio owner Ken Hamann produced. Maduri later told Scott that Wild Cherry was a "cross between Grand Funk (Railroad) and the Average White Band." An intriguing mash-up, indeed.

Mike Belkin was Sweet City president. Jules Belkin was secretary-treasurer. Joey Porrello, the former leader of Joey and the Continentals, was national promotion director. Steve Popovich, then vice president of artists and repertoire for Epic Records, told Scott "Cleveland is the most musically active city in the country right

LINER NOTES...................

A Royal Pain

Mike Belkin's view can be jaundiced. To him, Sly and the Family Stone was a "major, major pain in the ass that didn't give a shit about anything except getting drunk, getting high."

Belkin became involved with the large San Francisco band when Los Angeles promoter Ken Roberts called him, looking to book an open date. There was one available; the band played Public Auditorium on

August 9, 1969, sharing a bill with the Box Tops and the Sir Douglas Quintet.

"It was a mistake," Belkin says.

"The band would get there, most of the time on time," he says. "They would do their sound check. After the sound check, he (Sly) would go into his dressing room and bring everybody with him and lock the door and get high."

That date "was not a good experience because he made the people wait, they weren't allowed to open the outside doors, and I was in the building being pissed off," says Belkin. He urged Roberts to let people in, saying, "we don't want any kind of damages or any fighting. What finally happened was I pounded on their dressing room door, I was yelling, and told Kenny, get their asses out and on stage. We need to let people in." Belkin didn't care about the show itself, just about getting the band onstage "and out of the building." The doors finally opened.

Belkin did a few more dates with Sly Stone, who at least once "ended up sleeping in his car."

now. Five years ago, they would have laughed if you said that." Popovich, wrote Scott, "was instrumental" in signing the two-year Sweet City-Epic contract.

With the fast-track release of "Play That Funky Music" and Sweet City's debut mere weeks away, the late March announcement heralded the label as the fifth "division" of the Belkin empire, then located at 28001 Chagrin Place in Woodmere. The other four divisions were Belkin Productions; Belkin Personal Management, with the James Gang, Joe Vitale, Wild Cherry, Doug Sahm and the Michael Stanley Band among its clients; BEMA Publishing Co.; and Belkin-Maduri Productions, with Maureen McGovern, a Youngstown singer who hit No. 1 in 1973 with the Maduri-produced single "The Morning After," and the Cleveland Chamber Music Society among its clients.

Sweet City's brain trust, from left, Carl Maduri, Mike Belkin and Ron Alexenburg, head of Epic Records.

A Sweet City picnic at Mike Belkin's house. Michael Belkin is at lower left, Lisa Belkin is at top left, Rob Parissi in white is at center, Mark Avsec is fifth from top right, and Mike Belkin is bottom right next to dog.

"That was Carl's baby," Belkin says of McGovern, adding, "she was a pain in the ass." So was Wild Cherry leader Parissi, says Belkin, adding that in his view, Parissi had authority issues. Parissi also constantly griped about the difficulties of life on the road.

Cleveland Gets Funky

Wild Cherry opened for the New York Dolls at the Agora and for the Average White Band at the Coliseum. It also opened for The Isley Brothers, a soul group signed to another Epic-related label, in New York City. That match made for some unique staging challenges. In 2005, Popovich, who passed away in 2011, told this story:

"Carl Maduri brought me 'Play That Funky Music,' by Wild Cherry. A couple million albums and a million and a half singles. Still sells today. We couldn't put their picture on the cover because lead singer Bobby Parissi was white. That's why the cover has a photo of lips biting into a bright red cherry. They had a gig in New York opening for the

Isley Brothers, I talked to Carl Maduri about getting some black faces in that band, so we put four black guys in the horn section. The opening night of the tour was at Madison Square Garden. There were 20,000 people waiting for the Isley Brothers and Wild Cherry, which was a black hit at that time, and no one had ever seen them live. The guys walked out; it's dark and the crowd's on

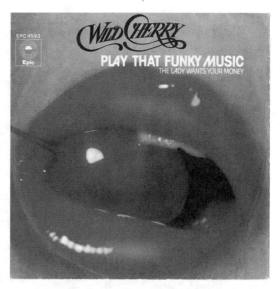

The legendary 45 single, released in April 1976, and distributed by Epic Records.

their feet going nuts, and Bobby Parissi walks out, the guy who wrote and sang that song, and it seemed everybody sat down. They played, and at the end they played 'Funky Music,' and everybody dug it. But it was a hard sell."

According to Mark Avsec, who played keyboards with Wild Cherry on tour, the band did dates with Earth Wind & Fire, Michael Jackson, Stevie Wonder, the Commodores, and Rufus with Chaka Khan, among others. Sounds like a tour made in heaven—a big hit, a whirlwind tour with the biggest names in music. Not exactly.

"Probably the worst tour that I managed was Wild Cherry, when they first went out on tour," says Belkin. "The song was an instant smash; it was instantaneous, so we had to get them out in front of the audience, put the band together, whatever it took to get them out on the road. The black audience was there to see the Isley Brothers and to see this new band with a big hit; they had no idea they were white. When they first went on tour the band was all white. After the first two or three days, to make it so the audience could relate to the white

Q made dance-floor waves with its 1977 single "Dancin' Man."

band, we hired four (black) horn players and they were onstage with the band. That was a very strange tour."

It was one in which Belkin took to disliking Parissi, too. "I always hope that whenever all is over and done with the artists that I manage, they have some money they've put away, so they don't have to get out on the street and beg for money. Parissi used to spend like mad. I tried to get him to save money, but every couple of months I'd see him drive into the parking lot with a new Cadillac.

"I didn't like the money he was spending and not saving. I'm also supposed to be advising him in different areas, and getting paid for it."

"Play That Funky Music" was by far the biggest Sweet City hit, though La Flavour's "Mandolay," written by Avsec, did very well, as did Steve Carlisle's theme song from the TV show "WKRP in Cincinnati." But by 1980, when Carlisle's tune was released, distribution of Sweet City had shifted from Epic to MCA, the label for which Iris and the Cruisers eventually recorded.

LaFlavour scored with "Mandolay" in 1979.

Before it faded in the early '80s, Sweet City released three Wild Cherry albums, along with 12-inch extended-play recordings by groups spanning La Flavour, the B.E. Taylor Group (in which Iris played), Q's dance-floor hit "Dancin' Man," and a disco tune called "Subway" by Samona Cooke, Sam Cooke's daughter.

But Sweet City wasn't the only soul game in town. At the time of the Sweet City announcement in the *Plain Dealer*, Avsec also was cit- .

From left: John "Sly" Wilson, the late Scott "Slick" Pittman and Jerome "Wicked" Pratt. Sly, Slick & Wicked recorded one single, "All I Want is You," for Sweet City Records.

ed as keyboardist for the Sweet City Band featuring ex-O'Jays drummer Jackie Cooper. That band is said to have signed to its namesake label, suggesting how much the Cleveland venture wanted to tell its own Motown-style success story. Cleveland was, indeed, a focus of recording activity, the *Plain Dealer's* Scott suggested in a December 24, 1976, article. This one focused on the soul style embodied in the new Sounds of Cleveland label.

Formed by original members of the O'Jays, Sounds of Cleveland was a short-lived imprint with offices on Miles Avenue. O'Jay Walter Williams sidestepped Scott when she asked him whether SOC would compete with Sweet City. "Competition is good for Cleveland. That's what our country is built on," he told Scott. "We don't have a corner on any market."

As for Sweet City, Belkin says it "has been a successful endeavor. We did not spend as much time as we should have finding new talent. However, it was a financial success due to 'Play that Funky Music,' which has sold millions of CDs and singles and is still selling."

'Funky Music' Scores Again

For a time, Sweet City looked like it would last. That was Wild Cherry time, both in the late 1970s and at the start of the '90s, when Robert M. Van Winkle, under the name Vanilla Ice, gave "Play That Funky Music" a big new boost and a second commercial life with an unauthorized take of Parissi's tune. The Ice version sold very, very well, hitting charts all over the world. You can almost hear Belkin laughing in disbelief over the outcome of Ice's boneheaded decision.

"The best part financially was when Vanilla Ice re-recorded 'Play That Funky Music' without getting permission from Sweet City. I ended up suing them and winning the lawsuit," says Belkin. "I think he (Vanilla Ice) sold 10 million

Mike Belkin and former Cleveland Mayor Carl Stokes.

albums." BEMA Music and co-publisher RWP (for Robert W. Parissi) sued Vanilla Ice, his management and his record company in October 1991 for copyright infringement. Besides Vanilla Ice, the defendants included SBK Music (a member label of the EMI Group), Ichiban Records, EMI Records and EMI Music. The New York Times called the Ice track a "rap update" of the original; *Billboard* called it an adaptation. Whatever the tag, it was a rip-off. Not only did it surface on Vanilla Ice's major-label debut, "To the Extreme," it also made it onto his "Extremely Live" follow-up. A Top 10 hit, it surfaced in many formats, from cassette to 12-inch. The civil suit sought $6 million in compensatory damages.

In an April 2013 interview with the Tampa Bay Times, Parissi said Vanilla Ice told people he'd written the tune. "Things like that make me laugh," Parissi said. "He paid me almost a million dollars. He was

A SPECIAL BOND

Mike Belkin and Mark Avsec

Mark Avsec, during the Wild Cherry years.

Mike Belkin and Mark Avsec's friendship goes way back. Avsec is a successful attorney on whom Belkin relies to this day for business advice. Belkin, according to Avsec, is like a second father to the musician-turned-lawyer. But before he was a successful attorney, Avsec was a talented and highly credited musician and songwriter:

• *Avsec wrote "She Don't Know Me," a track on Bon Jovi's first album. It is the only song on a Bon Jovi album not at least co-written by a member of the band.*

• *Avsec, Mason Ruffner and Alan Greene co-wrote "Angel Love (Come for Me)," a hit off the 2010 Santana "comeback" album, "Supernatural." Avsec and Greene (and drummer Kevin Valentine, a future Cruiser) are alumni of Breathless, the Mike Belkin-managed band Jonah Koslen formed after leaving the Michael Stanley Band. Ruffner, a Texas guitarist, used to be managed by Mike Belkin and even lived for some time at the Belkin home in Novelty.*

• *Avsec released albums in 1985 and 1988 under the name A Cellarful of Noise. The latter, "Magnificent Obsession," says "a great big thank you to Mike Belkin!" on the back cover.*

From left: Mike Belkin, Michael Stanley, Mark Avsec and a seated Donnie Iris.

wrong. I got 85 percent of everything he made on it. He made it gold. I was suing him all the time. At one time, MTV asked me, 'Don't you hate him?' I said, 'No: I want to adopt him.' "

Belkin liked owning a label when Wild Cherry was hitting big, but otherwise, he was largely hands-off. "Carl was really, for lack of a better term, the operating partner as far as the record company was concerned," Belkin says. "I was the operating partner on the manage-ment side." It was a partnership that would unravel.

The two drifted apart in the 1980s after the Belkin-Maduri Or-ganization signed Iris to an agreement calling on Iris to provide one album a year to Carousel Records, a custom imprint of MCA, for the term of a contract that ran from the spring of 1979 to the fall of 1981.

Sweet City and Midwest National, another Maduri partnership that led to the release of the first Iris and the Cruisers album, were Belkin's key forays into record label ownership. He's been involved with other labels including EMI, Epic and its affiliate CBS Associated, ABC Dunhill, and MCA as a manager but not as an owner.

As for Sweet City, it served as a meeting place for Iris and Avsec, the kingpins of what would become Iris and the Cruisers, a successful pop band that scored several hits in the '70s and '80s. Iris did background singing for Parissi's group. Their Wild Cherry tenure was in 1978 and 1979, and they joined forces at Jeree Records, a New Brighton, Pennsylvania studio where Wild Cherry was recording and Donnie Iris and the Cruisers recorded their first three albums.

Cruisers Time

Long before his Wild Cherry gig, Iris wrote and sang lead on "The Rapper," an earworm rhythm 'n' blues tune by the Pittsburgh band Jaggerz that became a No. 2 hit in 1970. A screamer and a belter, Iris pours his soul into his performances, particularly live ones. According to his website, donnieiris.com, Avsec was a big fan of "The Rapper." The stars were definitely aligning.

"Mike and Carl were behind us to go into the studio and record but we had to put a band together, which we did," Iris recalls. Next to join following the Avsec-Iris core: drummer Kevin Valentine, fresh off Jonah Koslen's band Breathless. Next up: an impressive bass player, Albritton McClain, from the Oxford, Ohio area. And since the rhythm guitar slot was filled with Iris, the last hole to plug was lead guitar. The nascent Cruisers scored a coup when they poached Marty Lee, who Iris says "blew me away," from an Erie, Pennsylvania band called The Pulse. Iris pitched Lee, whose real last name is Hoenes, by saying, "Look, we're doing a session at Jeree Records, I love the way you play. You want to come and do the session? He said yes.

"As soon as we went into the studio we knew we had something. We had a good band," Iris says. But it was a band Belkin wasn't quite ready to manage. That had to wait until the group's signature tune, "Ah! Leah!" began its chart ascent. "When the record started doing something, Mike became our manager and Carl Maduri became our executive producer; he was the executive producer through our recording session," Iris says.

Belkin Productions staff photo from around 1980, center row, from left: Jules Belkin, Mike Belkin, Carl Maduri, Jim Marchyshyn, and Jim Fox.

When "Ah! Leah!" began hitting on radio stations as far south as St. Louis and Dallas, Belkin began to take notice, Iris suggests. Chris Maduri, Carl's son and vice president of promotion and artist relations at Sweet City, convinced WMMS to play it. It also aired over Pittsburgh station WDVE and WBCN in Boston.

Avsec amplifies, attesting to the impact radio used to have: "If Kid Leo played 'Ah! Leah!' at 5:20 drive time on Friday night, the entire market heard it, so when we played a club, everybody would be there. Nowadays there is no radio that has that kind of filtering power because everything is so fragmented, so the market for a new band isn't necessarily listening to 'MMS; they may be coming home, watching YouTube or video games. And nobody's making money on music."

In the 1970s and early '80s, however, labels had cash and promotional budgets and "would look for artists to spend that money on," Avsec says. Belkin could bring Breathless to a label and "they would take a shot," using up their budgets, "and if one of them turned up

Mason Ruffner, left, and his manager, Mike Belkin.

with 'Hotel California' or Boston or Wild Cherry, you just paid for the building for the whole year."

Iris's voice, topping the vocal stack that makes "Ah! Leah!" indelible, grew loud enough for Belkin to take notice. Belkin had operated similarly with the James Gang and the Michael Stanley Band, taking over their management after they'd begun to establish themselves.

Belkin would serve as manager, but he also could act like a coach, urging more effective expression. Iris recalls that Belkin "thought I could do this a little better, that a little better, and he'd let me know about it. Not so much criticize, but he'd try to make me better. I remember singing a song that I was pretty much keeping all to myself, I wasn't connecting with the audience the way I should. I don't remember what song it was, but he told me about it. 'Rather than keep your eyes closed on that song, involve the audience, look at them.' You could be as intense with a song looking at somebody rather than keeping it behind your eyelids."

When it comes to seeing the bigger picture from a band perspective, Belkin "wants to see some action before he sticks his nose in," Iris says. "He's not just going to dive in and say, you guys want to make this record, here's all this money. He's going to want to see some action before he really puts his heart and soul into it. Which he did after he saw what was happening with the record."

Belkin "had us in to talk about managing us, and we absolutely said yes," Iris recalls. "Everything was what we had hoped for—I can't really give you numbers because I don't remember them—but it was at least industry standard or better for management, and we knew he was a good manager. And he had a track record."

"You have to get a band that is willing to go out there and tour and go into record stores and sign the autographs; that was the key back then," says Belkin. Tours and albums, too, have been critical for all the bands he's managed.

"If they don't happen to have a record deal, I have to believe in my heart I can make a deal for them, and then have them record and be able to go out and play live dates and tour," Belkin adds. "There's got to be hunger and promise on the part of the band. Once you're established and you have a market for your music, it becomes a lot easier to be out there touring."

And there are bands that are created, like Breathless, a group Belkin says he built with singer-songwriter Jonah Koslen, fresh from the Michael Stanley Band.

"Jonah's a talented guy, and the guys who were already part of the band were talented musicians," says Belkin. "I felt that was a band that could be popular and I knew there were some good writers in the band, and it was just a matter of time before something big was going to happen." But the first album wasn't as successful "as we all had hoped," he says. (Breathless recorded two albums for EMI, in 1979 and 1980.)

Iris and the Cruisers, too, began to lose power when their third album, "The High and the Mighty," didn't do as well as its snazzier predecessors "King Cool" and "Back on the Streets." Iris says he doesn't think the songs were as good. And lawsuits hobbled the band, keeping too much of its attention and energy in the courtroom rather than the recording studio and the stage.

Bumps in the Road

Belkin and Maduri, who years ago were partners in a Key Biscayne, Florida, condominium, parted ways over a lawsuit with Carousel, when Belkin contended that Iris "was not being promoted properly." Belkin says Maduri wanted Iris signed to Carousel Productions because Maduri's friend, Rick Frio, owned Carousel. The upshot was that the former allies had a falling out; ultimately, Iris was signed to Carousel, even as Belkin continued to manage him. "There came a point after Carl and I had this disagreement where Donnie had to make a decision as to whom he wanted to continue to be managed by, and Donnie felt that I had more experience in the management business and he would continue with me," says Belkin. The Carousel lawsuit was the only time there was friction between them.

During the trial, Iris recalls, Belkin wore a beautiful, gray silk tie with a red rose in the middle. Iris loved the tie. "I had complimented him on that tie, told him how much I liked it, and at the end of the trial, he gave it to me."

Flattery works with the generous Belkin. Iris recalls a party he attended with Belkin, who was wearing a watch Iris coveted. "Again, I complimented him on the watch. Two days later it's in my mailbox," he says.

Avsec, meanwhile, shifted careers to law. He is a copyright, trademark and media lawyer and a principal at Cleveland law firm Benesch, Friedlander, Coplan & Aronoff.

Avsec decided he wanted to be a lawyer "because we went through this unfair lawsuit," he says. A Detroit man claimed Avsec and Iris had "stolen" his song—a song the two had never heard. The lawsuit was

Mason Ruffner with a very young Sam Belkin.

thrown out, but the band lost its shirt to attorneys' fees and expenses linked to having to be in court in Detroit.

In a March 2012 interview with the website gojimmygo.net, Avsec said he never heard the plaintiff's song, adding, "I blame the contingency-fee lawyers who took the case, trying to take a shot."

After that enervating lawsuit over authorship of "Ah! Leah," Avsec decided law would be his focus. Pop music is "a young person's game, so when you reach your 20s and 30s, I was the last in the band to give it up," says Avsec, who at the time was supporting a wife and two children. "At some point, you got to do something else because you're not trying to have a hit record all the time."

While that suit left Avsec frustrated with the music business, he also called it "the best thing that happened to me. Because I love copyright law—and I love my life now, being an intellectual property attorney, teaching at law schools and speaking—and I'm also still writing music and playing."

Iris and the Cruisers still perform together; Paul Goll replaced McClain on bass. And it packs houses that hold 700 to 2,000, particularly in its key cities of Pittsburgh and Cleveland. "The success there is that we're still together and Mike is still booking the band these great gigs," says Iris.

Avsec shares a positive perspective on Belkin. "Mike has come to be almost like a second father to me, a supporter, a real friend, and he's always been there for me and I'd like to think I've been there for him," says Avsec. "When I went through personal issues, he was always a great sounding board," adds Avsec, who has worked with all the artists Belkin manages, even augmenting the James Gang when its classic lineup reunited in the early 2000s.

"We both get up at 4 a.m.," says Avsec, calling Belkin a hard worker who doesn't even have to work but does. "I think he lives well; I think he's a great guy for me to look up to, which I do."

While Belkin is an astute businessman, "he also genuinely loves artists and respects artists. I think he's kind of enamored of people in art. He appreciates it.

"We come from the analog days when the music industry was a different industry, a different economy," says Avsec. "It all changed in 1999 with Napster, and that was after all of us had our careers. So now we play shows and it's very gratifying, but the most gratifying things for me are my long relationships, with Mike, with Donnie. We play shows now. We're still good. The guys still want to go in the studio and make records."

Belkin has always liked to present shows, too. While he focused on management starting at the tail end of the '60s, in the middle of the '70s, Belkin was about to score with a big idea, stepping up to the plate to hit one out of the park for a grand slam the world of rock had never seen.

Chapter 9

Grand Slam Rock 'n' Roll

I do believe the last seat is mine

Joe Vitale ~ *Roller Coaster Weekend*

Promoting concerts, managing bands, launching a record label; in the music business of that era, it must have seemed that Mike Belkin had covered all the bases. It turns out that he was only loading the bases in order to set up a grand slam. Mike Belkin knocked rock 'n' roll out of the park while escorting Cleveland into the major leagues of live performances and outdoor events. The headliner of these Belkin events, of course, was the World Series of Rock.

BELKIN
PRODUCTIONS
Present

ROLLING STONES
TOUR OF THE AMERICAS 75
THEIR ONLY APPEARANCE IN THIS AREA!
SAT., JUNE 14th • 2:30 PM
★ CLEVELAND STADIUM ★
special guests

TOWER OF POWER
J. GEILS

$10 ADVANCE GEN. ADM.   PLUS 50¢ TICKETRON CHARGE
DOORS OPEN (1:30 P.M.—PERFORMANCE RAIN OR SHINE!
TICKETS ON SALE NOW CLEVELAND—ALL SEARS,
ALL CLEVELAND TUX SHOPS & MAY CO.
(DOWNTOWN); AND ALL OHIO TICKETRON OUTLETS.
A LIMITED NUMBER OF TICKETS STILL REMAIN
NO TICKETS WILL BE AVAILABLE DAY OF SHOW
★ NO BOTTLES OR CANS ALLOWED IN STADIUM ★

An early World Series of Rock lineup.

This multi-year, multi-act line-up of 15 performances ran between 1974 and 1980 at Cleveland Municipal Stadium, the cavernous open-air arena that was home to the Cleveland Browns and Indians until the mid-1990s. While Belkin Productions set attendance records with the World Series of Rock, the events also presented singular logistical challenges.

The Rolling Stones drew 86,000 to a July 1, 1978, date also featuring Kansas and Peter Tosh, according to the *Cleveland Press.* Pink Floyd, on its "Animals" tour, drew 83,000 to the stadium on June 25, 1977, setting a record for the largest number of tickets sold for a one-act concert, the only single-act show of the series.

The World Series of Rock at Municipal Stadium followed on the heels of a series of Belkin Productions shows at the Akron Rubber Bowl, onetime home of the Zips, the University of Akron's football team. Starting in 1972, the Rubber Bowl provided a large, outdoor venue for virtually every popular band of the day: the Stones, Stevie Wonder, Chicago, the Allman Brothers and more.

Mike Belkin speaks of a 1972 Stones concert at the Rubber Bowl that started out tense but turned out well. A tense tone was set the night before the show when a small bomb was set and detonated be-

World Series of Rock Lineups

DATE	Players
June 23, 1974	The Beach Boys, Joe Walsh and Barnstorm, Lynyrd Skynyrd, REO Speedwagon
August 4, 1974	Emerson, Lake & Palmer, Climax Blues Band, James Gang
September 1, 1974	Crosby, Stills, Nash & Young, Santana, The Band, Jesse Colin Young
May 31, 1975	The Beach Boys, Chicago
June 14, 1975	The Rolling Stones, Tower of Power, The J. Geils Band, Joe Vitale's Madmen
July 11, 1975	Yes, Joe Walsh, Michael Stanley Band, Ace
August 23, 1975	Rod Stewart and Faces, Uriah Heep, Aerosmith, Blue Öyster Cult, Mahogany Rush
June 5, 1977	Ted Nugent, Todd Rundgren's Utopia, Nazareth, Southside Johnny and the Asbury Jukes
June 25, 1977	Pink Floyd
August 6, 1977	Peter Frampton, Bob Seger and the Silver Bullet Band, The J. Geils Band, Derringer
July 1, 1978	The Rolling Stones, Kansas, Peter Tosh
July 15, 1978	Electric Light Orchestra, Foreigner, Journey, Trickster
August 26, 1978	Fleetwood Mac, Bob Welch, The Cars, Todd Rundgren and Utopia, Eddie Money
July 28, 1979	Aerosmith, Ted Nugent, Journey, Thin Lizzy, AC/DC, Scorpions
July 19, 1980	Bob Seger and the Silver Bullet Band, The J. Geils Band, Eddie Money, Def Leppard

neath the stage. Although no one was injured, the incident set nerves on edge and colored the pre-concert atmosphere.

That July 11, Belkin picked up the Stones at the airport and drove with them to the stadium, with five Akron police cars running es-

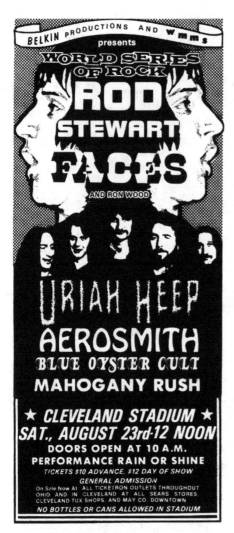

Finally, the rain ended as Rod Stewart took the stage.

cort. En route, the police scanner crackled with news of a riot at the site, but by the time the entourage arrived, the "riot" proved to be a handful of cops who overreacted to someone smoking dope on the infield.

The show did go on, however, according to Jane Scott's review in the *Plain Dealer*:

"A scream went up in the Akron Rubber Bowl that would make old-timers think of VJ Day in a boiler factory. Mick Jagger and the Rolling Stones had rolled down into the bowl in a van over the same hill used by the Soap Box Derby. This was what the 40,000 fans had been waiting for hours for, some even overnight."

Saying Stones front man Mick Jagger "sang every song with the energy of an encore," Scott also called the concert a "population zero nightmare," with teens, some smoking marijuana, "stretched knee to knee across the field."

The same year drew a Rubber Bowl show that was popular— but extremely unprofitable. The date was August 20, 1972, and the group was Chicago. Belkin Productions rented a Steinway piano and stretched canvas over four steel poles to create a makeshift stage. And then Belkin would be visited by every outdoor music promoter's worst demon: rain, and more rain, of biblical proportions.

Belkin offered a makeup date for fans holding the original tickets, but those were so soaked that it was hard to judge their authenticity. In the interim, however, Chicago had put out a very successful album, making the replay a winner.

Six years later, rain played a contributing role in another Belkin production. The Stones were back in Northeast Ohio for their July 1, 1978, World Series of Rock bill at Cleveland Stadium. An estimated 83,000 fans swarmed the arena and were rewarded with a Cleveland downpour.

"The rains came. Many fans huddled under blankets or plastic wraps," Scott wrote. "But the show was the most exuberant and exciting that Mick Jagger's group has brought here," Scott wrote of the July 1, 1978, bill.

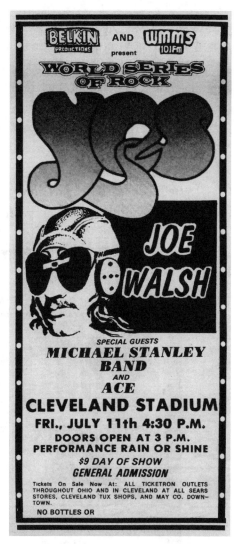

Mike Belkin called up local talent to lead off this World Series show.

As in life or rock 'n' roll, there were many such ups and downs at both the Akron and Cleveland stadiums. But in general, fans who attended World Series of Rock concerts overwhelmingly recall them with affection no matter their state of mind at the time. Belkin, who put together the bills, recalls the dates as massive undertakings with many more moving parts than smaller, more conventional presentations. The World Series of Rock generated major coverage and garnered mixed reviews, regularly making the front page. The series was arguably a big part of what made Cleveland such a renowned rock city in the 1970s and a contender for the Rock Hall in the 1990s.

A Winning Blend

To Belkin, sports and rock have a natural affinity. Besides the World Series of Rock and its obvious reference to baseball, Michael Stanley

The World Series of Rock found an alternative home in Richfield, Ohio, for the 1976 season.

would occasionally press his band into service to play baseball with visiting rock groups. Member of Belkin Productions would join the fun at many of those events.

The World Series of Rock, however, was in its own league. It all started in the stadium where the Cleveland Indians played. The date was June 23, 1974, and the headliners were the Beach Boys. Over six summers (there were no shows in 1976), these day-long events ran until July 19, 1980. Bob Seger and the Silver Bullet Band has the distinction of being the last players on the field when the Series drew to a close.

Mike Belkin continued to cover all the bases with top mainstream bands like ELO and Foreigner.

Belkin could pack the stadium that, except for Opening Day, the Indians couldn't. During those seven seasons, the Tribe went 537-584, never finishing higher than fourth place in the old American League East division. In terms of attendance, the low point during that span came in 1978, when 800,584 attended Indians home games. By comparison, in 2016, Indians home games drew nearly 1.6 million in Progressive Field, a far smaller ballpark.

WMMS & BELKIN PRODUCTIONS WELCOME

World Series Of Rock Game III

IN CONCERT

FLEETWOOD MAC

CHRISTINE McVIE
STEVIE NICKS
MICK FLEETWOOD
LINDSEY BUCKINGHAM
JOHN McVIE

SPECIAL GUESTS

TODD RUNDGREN'S UTOPIA
BOB WELCH   CARS
NEW DATE
SAT., AUGUST 26 — 4:00 P.M.
CLEVELAND LAKEFRONT STADIUM
GATES OPEN 2 P.M.
NO BOTTLES OR CANS PLEASE

TICKETS: $12.00 ADVANCE, $15.00 DAY OF SHOW, PLUS $.60 TICKETRON SERVICE CHARGE. **PLENTY OF GOOD TICKETS STILL AVAILABLE,** ON SALE NOW AT ALL TICKETRON LOCATIONS IN OHIO & PENN. **REFUNDS AVAILABLE AT POINT OF PURCHASE THROUGH AUGUST 20. TICKETS FOR ORIGINAL AUGUST 5 DATE HONORED.**
LISTEN TO WMMS FOR ALL WORLD SERIES OF ROCK INFO

This 1978 concert was originally scheduled for August 5, but Lindsay Buckingham's illness forced its rescheduling to August 26.

Admission to that first concert was $7 in advance, $8 at the gate. Supporting the Beach Boys were "undercard" acts Joe Walsh and Barnstorm, and "special guests" Lynyrd Skynyrd and REO Speedwagon. Clearly, this was no regular season show, as any of the warm-up bands would typically be a headliner.

By the final show, general admission tickets to the Seger date, which, like the others, began around noon, cost $12.50. Also on that World Series finale were Belkin favorite the J. Geils Band, Eddie Money, and Def Leppard, making its North American debut in Cleveland.

No World Series of Rock concerts took place at the stadium in 1976 because damage to the field caused by fans forced Belkin Productions to move mega productions like this to the Richfield Coliseum. The series restarted in 1977 after stadium groundskeepers applied a field cover consisting of plywood and outdoor carpeting.

Chris Jacobs, a drummer and businessman from Rocky River, saw seven World Series shows; one that stands out for him—for a bizarre reason—took place on August 4, 1974, featuring the James Gang, the Climax Blues Band, and headliner Emerson, Lake & Palmer. Jacobs'

This show was notoriously out of control and ultimately led to the demise of the World Series of Rock.

most vivid memory of it is the guy sitting next to him reading the weighty, classic novel *Moby Dick* throughout the concert. Talk about being lost in your own world.

Jacobs also attended the last World Series of Rock show of 1975. The date was August 23, the tickets $10 in advance, $12 day of show. The undercard was Mahogany Rush, Blue Oyster Cult, Aerosmith, and Uriah Heep. The main attraction was Rod Stewart and the Faces, on their last tour. Jacobs says Stewart's entrance, in a green suit, to the accompaniment of David Rose's "The Stripper," was sensational. He and a friend had gotten to Cleveland Stadium early to camp out on the field. It rained. And it rained. And it rained. Everyone was soaked. WMMS, meanwhile, was broadcasting music, and when it aired "Here Comes the Sun," the skies suddenly cleared, as if on cue.

"The drizzle stopped and the show started and it was one of the greatest entrances I've ever seen by a rock star."

"All the bands were great, but when we left, the field was destroyed," littered with blankets and sleeping bags, Jacobs says. "It was crappy the rest of the year," he adds, noting "eventually they got smart and covered the field with plywood," laying Astroturf over that.

A Mixed Bag

According to numerous accounts like this, the World Series of Rock could be a blast. It also could be a mess. It was equally celebrated for music and intoxication.

Is Belkin proud of it? "I don't think we had any major accidents, and ultimately the end result was we got people to come to downtown Cleveland, people went to Cleveland Stadium, and there was a minimal number of injuries that occurred through the series."

Attending one of the shows could be scary, however. Consider the experience of Michael Norman, a fan who covered rock for the *Plain Dealer* for a time during the 2000s. He and his high school girlfriend went to the August 6, 1977, show featuring Derringer, the J.

Geils Band, Bob Seger and the Silver Bullet Band, and headliner Peter Frampton. And contrary to the popular maxim, getting there was not half the fun. In fact, it was no fun at all.

"I remember standing in line outside the stadium waiting for them to open those old corrugated gates," Norman recalls. "I had a white Styrofoam cooler filled with beer and wine because in those days you could bring whatever you wanted into the venues. Everybody was geared up to rush in as soon as they raised the gates because with the festival seating, the faster you ran in, the better your seat. But the crush of people was intense as the time neared and I remember the pressure was so great that the cooler exploded against my chest just as they raised the gate. Then everyone rushed inside, but people were falling and it got very dangerous because the interior of the stadium concourse had a permanent metal maze of rows meant to direct people toward old-fashioned turnstiles. People were being crushed against the metal tubing and some of them got flipped over them and almost trampled. I just remember grabbing my girlfriend by the hand and telling her to push with me and not to stop no matter what. Luckily, we were near the turnstile and got through, but it was harrowing."

Others, however, had a more relaxed experience. Take Pat Randle, a Lakewood woman who attended the Crosby, Stills, Nash &

The World Series of Rock took monumental setup efforts.

The field of Cleveland Municipal Stadium, home of the Cleveland Indians and Cleveland Browns, had to be covered with plywood and Astroturf for many of the shows.

Young reunion tour at the old stadium, a concert that also featured Santana, The Band, and Jesse Colin Young. Staged on September 1, 1974, this was her second World Series show.

"Those bands were pretty mellow," Randle recalls. "I went with my friend. We took home-baked cookies, traded some for a little pot and a better place to sit in the festival seating. I remember amazing harmonies and bliss!"

A Grounds-up Challenge

Belkin Productions and FM powerhouse WMMS were media sponsors for the World Series of Rock. Belkin Productions rented the stadium on a show-by-show basis from then-Cleveland Browns owner Art Modell, who in turn leased the stadium from the city of Cleveland.

Belkin put together the bills. "That involved having an agreement among all the bands on the bill—who went first, who went last, how much time they were given," he says. "You have to have the agreement from all the bands if you want all the bands to be playing. When you have one or two that are stronger overall, you have to explain that to the other bands." Given the outsized egos of some performers, that explaining could be a major league feat of its own.

The process starts with picking a headliner and finding availability "for not only them but for the other acts that would be on the bill." If the headliner is available and willing to play the desired date, "you find out the other bands you felt were strong enough to make a strong lineup," Belkin says. "If they had played in the area before you knew how many tickets they could sell," he adds.

WMMS & BELKIN PRODUCTIONS WELCOME

THE 1980 WORLD SERIES OF ROCK

THIS SATURDAY!!

Bob Seger & The Silver Bullet Band

And Special Guest Stars

J. GEILS BAND
EDDIE MONEY
DEF LEPPARD
SATURDAY, JULY 19 - 4:00
CLEVELAND LAKEFRONT STADIUM

GATES OPEN AT 2:00 STADIUM LOTS OPEN AT 6:00 THE MORNING OF THE CONCERT. STADIUM AREA OPENS AT 8:00. NO CANS OR BOTTLES PERMITTED.

TICKETS: $12.50 Advance, $15.00 Day Of Show, On sale now at all Ticketron Outlets in Ohio and Pennsylvania, and at Stadium Gate B on the day of the event. All Ticket holders enter through Gates A & D.

Buy your tickets from authorized ticket outlets ONLY. People selling tickets on the street ALWAYS have counterfeits.

Listen to **WMMS** 101 FM for all World Series Of Rock information

The World Series of Rock went out with a bang in 1980.

For example, Belkin first secured the availability of the Rolling Stones for a June 14, 1975, World Series of Rock bill also featuring Tower of Power, J. Geils Band, and Joe Vitale's Madmen. The Stones didn't have a preference for who else played but had to OK the entire lineup. The same process pertained to the other bands, though they were easier to negotiate with because they were happy to get the exposure that came with the headliner.

But with the addition of more artists, the harder the process became. There was a lot of back-and-forth, adjusting schedules and lineups to accommodate demands and egos. A promoter also had to deal with agents and managers. "It's a complex situation," Belkin says. "Those World Series of Rock concerts were very time-consuming and not just because of the actual performance time."

Among other issues: Belkin Productions had to know when to start advertising and how long to advertise for each concert, "because there is overlap between the concerts," so they would advertise two to three months in advance.

There was also literal groundwork. "Just to set up the field and the stage took quite a long time and a multitude of labor with stagehands," says Belkin. "You had to deal with police, you had to deal with sound companies and lighting companies. It required a whole lot of technical situations in daytime and nighttime, and you had to make sure that it would sound good all over the stadium."

The headliner was always the key. Managing one of the participating bands also helped, as in the case of the James Gang, the Michael Stanley Band, Joe Walsh and Barnstorm, Walsh solo, and Vitale's Madmen. All were or are managed by Belkin.

The ultimate difficulty arose from a situation not even Belkin could manage. The city—run by Mayor George Voinovich—ultimately shut down the World Series of Rock for safety reasons, a decision that still rankles Belkin. "The city says, look, it's not safe to be down there, no more concerts, what are you going to do? You've heard that saying, you can't fight city hall," he says.

What apparently convinced city leaders to pull the plug on the World Series of Rock was the July 28, 1979, show featuring Scorpions, AC/DC, Thin Lizzy, Journey, Ted Nugent, and Aerosmith.

The website of classic rock FM radio station WNCX said that show was "noted for its intensity."

"Since these shows were all general admission, fans would camp outside the old Lakefront Stadium to get the best possible seats thus becoming a target for criminals," he continued. "There were at least eight robberies reported and numerous incidents of theft, vandalism and gang violence. The media reported that five people were shot including one fatality. Also, one other fatality allegedly occurred inside when someone climbed and then fell off the backstop. Belkin Productions then rescheduled a concert for August 19th that year and, under pressure from city officials, canceled it altogether. Putting the

Throngs attended Belkin Productions festivals in Cleveland's Flats entertainment district.

Faith Hill at a Pepsi country music festival in Berea, Ohio.

blame mostly on lack of safety, the last World Series of Rock took place on July 19, 1980."

A Feast of Festivals

Though the World Series of Rock passed into history, the complexity of Belkin presentations carried over to the world of festivals. The most famous was the Great American Rib Cook-Off, which debuted in 1992. Other Belkin Productions festivals included a country music festival with Pepsi as sponsor, and the Ohio Lottery $3 million Hole in One. Belkin's flair for showmanship was alive, well and coming to life in different forms at different events.

"Always something bigger, always something better," was Belkin's mantra, whether that applied to rock shows or festivals, notes Barry Gabel, Belkin Productions marketing director and now senior vice president of marketing and sales at Live Nation.

Like the World Series of Rock, the festivals also largely had their day and their place in history.

In February 2016, Live Nation, which bought Belkin Productions in 2001, canceled the Great American Rib Cook-Off, saying it was time to put it on pause and that competition from similar events had led to over-saturation of the market.

Gabel, who handled the rib cook-off for Live Nation, said Live Nation would focus on events other than the rib festival held over Memorial Day weekend at Jacobs Pavilion and the Nautica Entertainment Complex on the Flats West Bank.

Mike's son Michael booked the "musical elements" for the cook-off. Michael's sister, Lisa, who worked part-time for Belkin Productions in the '90s, handled the carnival games. "I would have to find people to work all these shifts, which wasn't so bad when my kids were old enough to have friends who could come down and work as well," she says, adding she wasn't involved in festival production per se. Eventually, their cousin Jamie also came to focus on the festivals as well as on some concert production, according to Michael.

"What drove the event was the music," says Mike Belkin, who conceived of the cook-off. "Each one was profitable, but it kind of slowly lost its charm." Still, there was more to the rib cook-off than tunes and crowds enjoying great ribs and great sauce.

Over the years, that cook-off changed locale, date, and forms of entertainment. Belkin recalls an early iteration.

The 2000 Taste of Cleveland Festival featured Alice Cooper, top, and Prodigal Son.

The Monkees, from left: Peter Tork, Davey Jones and Mickey Dolenz at one of the festivals.

The festivals were all family-friendly events that became an annual tradition for many Clevelanders.

At first, the rib cook-off was a uniquely aquatic event, a grueling one that ran from noon to 11 p.m. on four or five consecutive days.

Credit Belkin's inner sportsman.

"I came up with the idea that we would do a hole-in-one on the water and the winner who was able to get the ball closest to the hole would get a $1,000 cash prize," says Belkin. "We built a floating green and used floating golf balls and we ran it during the day. People paid to get X amount of balls." Businesspeople came down during lunch to try their luck, and there was one winner per cook-off.

Belkin Productions positioned a sign next to the Ninth Street Pier, listing winners and near-winners by name, along with a record of the distance from where the ball had stopped at the hole. A two-person Belkin Productions crew ran a small, single-engine boat around the area, picking up golf balls floating in the Cuyahoga River that had missed the desired mark.

The Belkin festivals helped revive Cleveland's Flats District along the Cuyahoga River.

Other festivals Belkin Productions staged were Taste of Cleveland, which ran from 1999 to 2010; Kidsfest, staged intermittently between 1992 and 2006; Oktoberfest, in 2004 and 2005; the High School Rock Off, starting in 1997; and X-Fest, in Dayton, Ohio, from 1996 to 2010.

Belkin Productions would tie Kidsfests to a local hospital and the country music festivals would involve co-sponsors like a local supermarket chain and a country music radio station. Admission cost to these festivals included entertainment, and their biggest enemy was rain.

"We were rained out for days at a time," Belkin says, adding festivals were drawn out. "I used to stay to the end, until 11:30, and I used to get there an hour early. Those were long days."

Landlord Mike

On the personal front, Belkin has owned some choice real estate.

Over time, he owned an apartment in New York City and several condominiums in Key Biscayne, Florida. From the 1970s through 2001, he was partners with his brother in that New York apartment

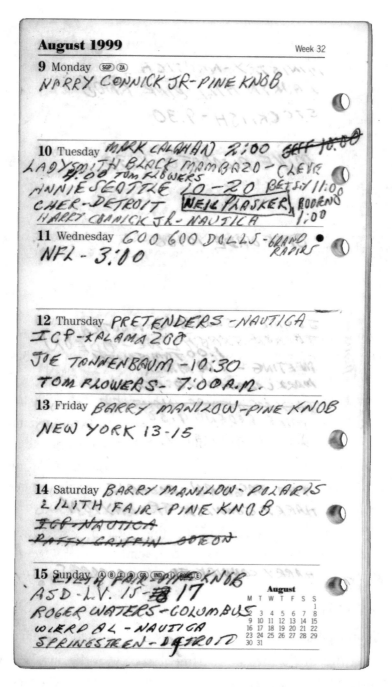

After more than 30 years, Mike Belkin still kept a hand-written event calendar, but changed to a more compact, refillable page format.

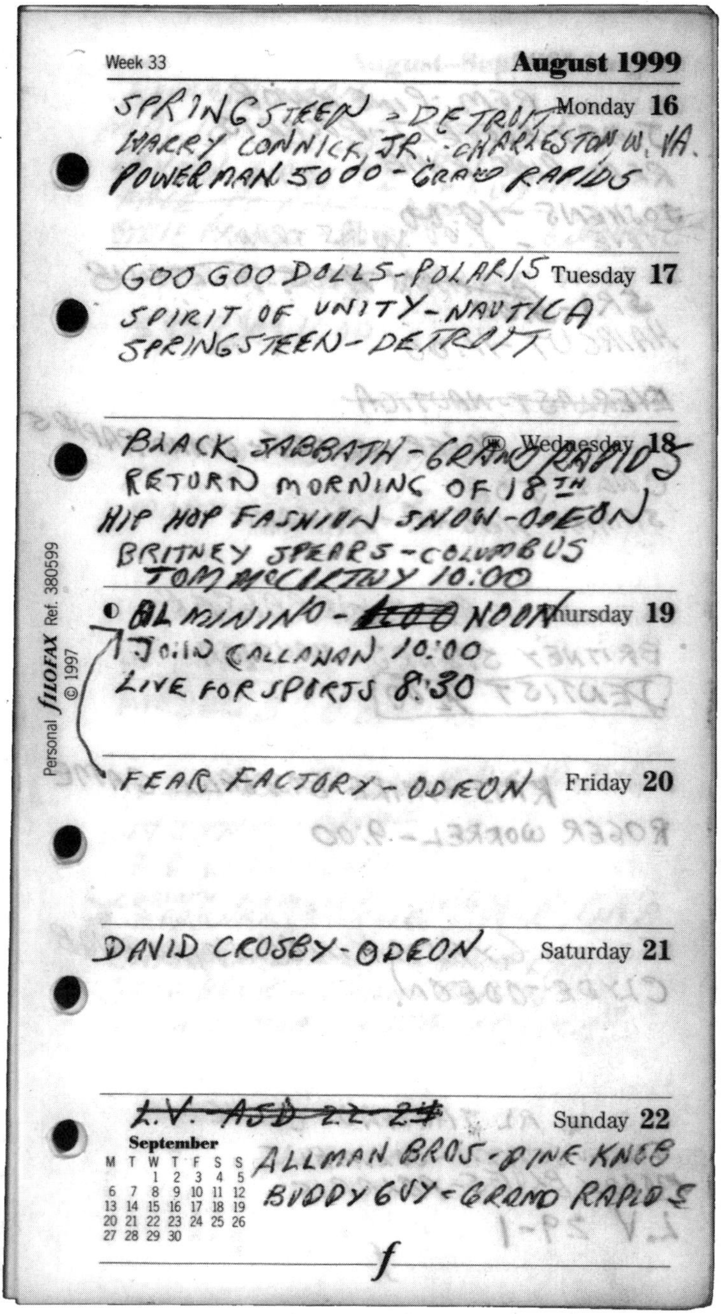

Week 33 **August 1999**

SPRINGSTEEN - DETROIT Monday **16**
HARRY CONNICK, JR. - CHARLESTON W, VA.
POWERMAN 5000 - GRAND RAPIDS

GOO GOO DOLLS - POLARIS Tuesday **17**
SPIRIT OF UNITY - NAUTICA
SPRINGSTEEN - DETROIT

BLACK SABBATH - GRAND RAPIDS Wednesday **18**
RETURN MORNING OF 18ᵀᴴ
HIP HOP FASHION SHOW - ODEON
BRITNEY SPEARS - COLUMBUS
TOM McCARTNY 10:00

AL NINO - NOON Thursday **19**
JOHN CALLANAN 10:00
LIVE FOR SPORTS 8:30

FEAR FACTORY - ODEON Friday **20**

DAVID CROSBY - ODEON Saturday **21**

L.V. ASD 22 24 Sunday **22**

September
M T W T F S S
1 2 3 4 5
6 7 8 9 10 11 12
13 14 15 16 17 18 19
20 21 22 23 24 25 26
27 28 29 30

ALLMAN BROS - PINE KNOB
BUDDY GUY - GRAND RAPIDS

f

Personal *FILOFAX* Ref. 380599 © 1997

at West 57th Street and Sixth Avenue, and he and Sweet City record label executive Carl Maduri co-owned a condo in Key Biscayne; independently, Belkin also owned four others in that Miami suburb, one condo at a time.

"I would try and upgrade, so every time we were down there if we saw something that was priced right for us and nicer, we would try and sell the one we were in and move into the larger, nicer one," says Belkin. The experience in Florida was not without risk, however. Belkin recalls a harrowing experience in August 1992, when Hurricane Andrew blew out a bathroom wall into a hallway. "I remember Annie carrying (their son) Sam up the stairs," out of harm's way, he recalls.

Belkin sold his last Key Biscayne condo in 2012 after Sam graduated from the University of Miami. Although he never lost on a

condo sale and did well on most, he regrets selling that one: "The view from that last one would take your breath away," he says. "The dining room and living room were just one long room, and on each end, there was a deck, so one overlooked the ocean and the other one overlooked Biscayne Bay and the skyline of Miami."

As of 2017, Belkin's only personal property was his house in rural Geauga County.

Mike Belkin, left, with best friend Harry Eisner in Acapulco.

Jules Belkin, left, and Mike Belkin flank Paula Abdul.

Clubman Mike

On the commercial front, Belkin has been involved in several real estate ventures.

While Belkin Productions booked all sorts of venues, from clubs in Ohio and Michigan to Public Auditorium and Music Hall, the Richfield Coliseum and, occasionally, Blossom Music Center, it didn't own one in its hometown until 1994, when it bought the Odeon Concert Club. That nightclub in Cleveland's Flats could accommodate up to 1,000.

The Odeon is a nifty club, with great sightlines, comfortable seating, and good bills. Among the groups and rock stars that have played there are Metallica, Radiohead, Oasis, John Mayer, Soul Coughing, No Doubt, and Nine Inch Nails.

The Odeon wasn't the first commercial real estate in which Belkin had an interest, however. Early in his rock 'n' roll career, he owned

Belkin Productions logos, from 1978, left, and 1985.

part of Roy's, a restaurant in Los Angeles. The restaurant's principal was Roy Silver, who died in 2003. Silver managed talent such as Tiny Tim and other acts that Belkin Productions presented earlier. Belkin Productions also was part-owner of the Savoy, a tony venue that rock promoter Ron Delsener created in the old Hudson Theater on West 44th Street in midtown Manhattan at the start of the '80s.

"It was a beautiful club," Belkin recalls. "Leather banquettes, and we spent a lot of money fixing it up." Delsener reportedly sunk $1.5 million into the midtown club, which held 950 and lasted from 1981 to 1982. The Savoy opened with a sellout show by Cliff Richards, and Genesis and Olivia Newton-John played there among many others.

Pete Townshend was a frequent visitor to the Savoy. When Belkin asked the Who leader what he thought of the place, Townshend said it was beautiful, "but the problem is it's too nice and I don't think the young people are going to be comfortable in this place. And he was right."

Closer to home, Belkin says the Odeon, which Belkin Productions sold in 2006, wasn't beautiful, but it was successful. The club on Old River Road on the Flats East Bank closed shortly after Belkin Productions was sold in 2001 to SFX, a media conglomerate that shortly thereafter was sold to Clear Channel Communications.

In a 2006 article in the *Youngstown Vindicator*, Michael Belkin said Belkin Productions decided to shutter the Odeon because the club market was saturated and the House of Blues, in particular, offered stiff competition. Besides, Belkin Productions was shifting focus to larger venues.

"We're still obviously the primary presenter of entertainment at Quicken Loans (Arena) and Cleveland State University, Tower City Amphitheater, Scene Pavilion, (and) Playhouse Square," Belkin said, as reported by *Vindicator* correspondent John Benson. He also cited Belkin Productions interests in the Post-Gazette Pavilion and Chevrolet Amphitheatre at Station Square in Pittsburgh.

Tower City Amphitheater, renamed Time Warner Cable Amphitheater, closed in 2011 in connection with development of the JACK Cleveland Casino.

Larger-scale enterprises also figured in other Belkin Productions investments.

In partnership with Sunshine Promotions of Indianapolis, Belkin Productions built the Polaris Amphitheater, which opened in 1994, according to *Columbus Business First.*

The Belkins sold their portion of Polaris, later known as the Germain Amphitheater, to enable the sale of Sunshine Promotions to SFX in 1997. In 2001, SFX bought Belkin Productions for nearly $11 million.

SFX spent $2 billion in the last three years of the '90s acquiring promoters representing more than 120 clubs and amphitheaters, according to the *Los Angeles Times.* In August 2000, the radio aggregator Clear Channel Communications bought SFX for $2.9 billion in stock and $1.5 billion in assumed debt. In 2005, Clear Channel spun off its entertainment unit as Live Nation. Both Mike Belkin and his son, Michael, are Live Nation executives.

Winding Down

According to Belkin, "Jules wanted to sell and was not happy with the company structure and wanted to retire, which was fine with me.

I was working my ass off every day. I have never regretted selling the company, although I always enjoyed the special events."

The acquisition included Belkin Productions and all its branches, including a Michigan promotion company, the Belkin Concert Club, and Belkin's festival arm. As part of its strategy, SFX bought several other promoters and their assets at the same time.

"The money which was being offered was what I called 'stupid money,' " Belkin says—"an offer which almost all of the promoters accepted."

That same year, he and two associates founded Pinnacle Marketing, a sports merchandising firm. Two years later, Belkin, its president, and Richard Dickerson, Pinnacle's vice president, bought out Steven Kaufman, Dickerson's cousin and Pinnacle's secretary and another vice president.

"Richard and I felt there was a void in the market for a company that sold licensed college and professional apparel, headwear and hard goods to drug and grocery chains," Belkin says. "We were correct and have been partners and friends from that day—and successful."

He goes to work at Pinnacle virtually every day.

With the sale of Belkin Productions behind him, Belkin could refocus on sports, his earliest love, through the prism of business. At the same time, he could spend precious time collecting art and advocating for artists.

Belkin awakens in, and comes home to, a house brimming with creativity, beauty and art.

Chapter 10

An Eye for Beauty

She comes on like daylight softly creeping
Sneaking through the glass

Donnie Iris ~ *Sweet Merilee*

For years, Mike Belkin has collected the beautiful and the unusual. A discerning, dedicated art lover, he has amassed caches of sculptures, paintings, glass, and coins as well as limited-edition books on art, photography and rock 'n' roll; many of the books are so heavy they sit on substantial pedestals.

Enter the country home that Belkin and his wife, Annie, so comfortably occupy and you'll encounter inviting, modern furniture, the

Mike and Annie Belkin's comfortable rural home is filled with art.

saucy sculpture of a topless French maid, lamps that change colors, and elegant shelves bearing art glass.

Their urbane, playful house celebrates creativity and the artistic impulse. The house also helps mark the passage of time; clocks, some surreal, many high-tech, are all over the place, mounted on walls and perched on kitchen shelves.

Contemporary art glass, however, is the signature of this household. The glass collection includes the startling, deeply organic work of Paul Stankard, Henry Halem's boxed "environments," Steven Weinberg pieces aggressive with bubbles and gnarl, and William Carlson's glowing geometrics.

"I started collecting glass made by Tiffany," says Belkin, who embarked on this particular quest in the late '70s when he attended a Sotheby's auction. "I just have this fascination for reflective quality, for being able to hold something in my hand, to examine it, to take the magnifying glass and look at it closely. There's a magic to me with glass, (but it's) very hard for me to explain what that magic is."

Belkin's first true focus was 19th-century French paperweights, including ones by Baccarat. He also bought prints by the likes of Wil-

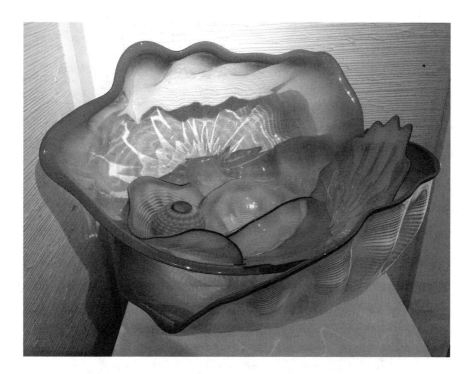

The organic forms of a bowl by Dale Chihuly.

LINER NOTES..................

Hello, Dali

Toward the end of its career, the James Gang decided it wanted to use a painting by Salvador Dali for the cover of "Newborn," its penultimate album, which dates from 1975. The Gang knew it needed permission, so Mike Belkin, the band's manager, contacted Dali's agent to arrange a meeting.

The Dali piece of interest was painted by the Catalan artist in 1943. It's titled "Geopoliticus Child Watching the Birth of the New Man." Created when World War II was at its height, it uneasily blends imagery of the collapse of the old order and the struggle attending the birth of a new one.

"Dali was in New York staying at a hotel, so we went to New York," Belkin recalls. "I flew into New York and went to the hotel, and he wasn't in his hotel room, but the representative was."

Puzzled, Belkin told the agent he'd flown in from Cleveland to meet Dali and get permission to use his painting for the James Gang album cover.

"He's not here right now, you can find him over at the Metropolitan Museum," the agent told him, so Belkin took a cab to the Met.

"He was in one of the galleries looking at the art, so I walked up to him and introduced myself. He didn't know anybody was going to come," Belkin says.

Dali was surprised. "I told him why I was there and he said to me, 'my representative will get back to you.' But he never did."

The James Gang used the painting anyway.

Dali was "a tall guy," says Belkin. "He was busy looking at the art. I was overwhelmed. This was Dali. The Gang was very proud of that cover."

From left: Paul Stankard, Dale Chihuly, Steven Weinberg, William Carlson.

lem de Kooning, Robert Motherwell and Claes Oldenburg, for aesthetic reasons as well as investments. He owns two candelabras designed by Salvador Dali. And over time, he purchased pieces by glass art superstar Dale Chihuly.

Belkin began seriously collecting contemporary art glass after Stankard took him to a museum of contemporary art glass in Millville, New Jersey, where Stankard's contemporary glass collection was on loan.

While his own talent for creating art is a self-proclaimed "big fat zero," Belkin certainly has an eye for it, in much the same way as he has an ear for rock 'n' roll. His interest in the field developed after college, and he learned about the art itself as well as the art market by reading auction catalogs and comparing estimates to sale prices. Once Annie joined his life, she, too, learned that same way.

"It's very eclectic," Belkin says of his collection. "Annie—and she's got good taste—likes pieces that are unusual; when we buy a piece of art, we need to agree on if we both like it.

"My glass art collection has grown, thanks to my wife," says Belkin. He also salutes "my four fantastic artist friends who have taught me about the art of glass and from whom I have been able to purchase their wonderful work."

Annie, too, loves art, particularly ceramics. Her husband, she says, is a "mighty, mighty collector—he's got it in his blood." He schooled her in the field, and while they have different interests, they agree on what to acquire and what to give away.

The two have bought art wherever they traveled, and they attend such key shows as Art Basel in Miami and the Sculpture Objects Functional Art and Design Fair, or SOFA, in Chicago.

"We saw how things were done," Annie says. "It was an education for me and it was fun."

The Belkins also have made some artists part of their extended family. Stankard, Carlson, Halem and Weinberg have frequented the same galleries, go to bat for each other, and value their friendship with the Belkins.

These artists speak of Belkin with affection, appreciation and gratitude. They value his warmth and business acumen and applaud his open-mindedness and generosity.

They also like the way he has let them into his life, sharing his rock 'n' roll largesse such as concert tickets and backstage passes. He also invites them to parties in his back yard and, in one case, enlisted the help of one at a festival Belkin produced.

Although Belkin never actually managed them, he assisted these artists in developing their careers and advised them on how to market and represent themselves commercially. When necessary and the time was right, he'd help them financially. Steadfastness and consistency were foundations of his approach.

Paul Stankard, left, and Mike Belkin in Florida.

Paul Stankard

Before he began collecting contemporary American art glass, Belkin had amassed collections of vintage beaded handbags and antique French paperweights. Once he began to gather up modern glass, however, he divested himself of those, shifting focus to glass art. It was Paul Stankard's work that attracted him from the beginning.

Stankard's complex, detailed paperweights and orbs come alive with stunningly realistic flamework glass plants, flowers and insects. In 2011, the artist told the *Akron Beacon Journal* that his focus was native flowers and "the cycle of life."

On one visit to Cleveland, Stankard and Belkin strolled out into Belkin's backyard and across a field that took them deep into nature. They admired the flowers there and Stankard created a piece commemorating their walk. Belkin has a "love of nature, a love of beauty," says Stankard, noting both are bird watchers.

Over the decades, the Belkins have commissioned several Stankard "collections," which range from four to eight pieces. Within the past 15 years, they have donated Stankard works to the likes of the

Paul Stankard's artwork is so vivid with detail it seems real.

Akron Art museum (the largest beneficiary); the Cleveland Museum of Art; the Huntington Museum of Art in Huntington, West Virginia; the Chrysler Museum of Art in Norfolk, Virginia; the Wheaton Arts and Cultural Center in Millville, New Jersey; the Bergstrom-Mahler Museum of Glass in Neenah, Wisconsin; the Hokkaido Museum of Modern Art in Sapporo, Japan; the Metropolitan Museum of Art in New York; and the Victoria and Albert Museum in London.

In 2011, the couple donated 64 Stankards to the Akron Art Museum, where they are installed in a permanent display case above the lobby. The Mike and Anne Belkin Collection of Paul Stankard Glass is the largest assortment of Stankard sculptures and paperweights in the world.

Belkin bought his first Stankard in 1981 for $770 (it would now be worth about $3,000, he says) at a Sotheby's auction. When he told his adviser he'd like to meet Stankard, Belkin called the man at his home in Mantua, New Jersey, and Stankard invited them up.

"He's a sweetheart, a very accommodating individual," Belkin says of Stankard. "He took us to his studio and we had lunch together, and the rest is history. We bonded and I helped him with the sales of some of his work."

Stankard, who speaks with the accent of his suburban Boston upbringing, vividly recalls the first time he met Belkin.

"I'll never forget—he pulled up in a limousine, and he was wearing a long leather coat," Stankard says. "He told me he was interested in art work and he would like to commission me to do some special pieces. There was a wonderful presence about him, he was very gracious."

On the spot, Belkin offered to write a $20,000 check as a commission for a "nice collection" of his work. "I was so excited when he left, I was dancing around my living room," Stankard says.

Upon completion of that first assortment, Belkin sent Stankard another $20,000 check. "It became a very, very beautiful friendship," Stankard says, and Belkin "evolved from patron to a beautiful family friend."

In one of their frequent morning telephone conversations, Belkin offered Stankard tickets to a U2 concert in Philadelphia, with guitarist Mason Ruffner opening. Belkin managed Ruffner.

Stankard told Belkin thanks, but he wasn't interested in the concert. But when he relayed that rejection to his family at dinner, "What are you talking about?" was the incredulous response. Ultimately, the whole Stankard pack went to the show, and they even received backstage passes. As for the concert itself, "I was afraid I was going to go deaf," Stankard says, chuckling. "It was off-the-charts noisy." Stankard's kids, of course, were thrilled.

Over the years, Belkin helped spread the word to other collectors and was instrumental in negotiating a deal for the book *Paul J. Stankard: Homage to Nature* by Ulysses Grant Dietz, published in 1996.

Venetian master Gianni Toso's Seder scene.

Henry Halem

Stankard helped Belkin, too, turning him on to Heller Gallery in New York and Habatat Galleries in suburban Detroit, respectively run by art dealers Douglas Heller and Ferdinand Hampson. Hampson gave Belkin a list of ten contemporary glass artists to track and collect, and Belkin began to "make very, very thoughtful purchases of contemporary glass," Stankard says.

He has stature in that community, too. Belkin is a Fellow of the Corning Museum of Glass in upstate New York, a former president of the Dallas-based Art Alliance for Contemporary Glass, and a member of the Contemporary Glass Center of America Board of Trustees, an advisory board to the Wheaton Arts and Cultural Center.

Belkin's early purchases included work by Henry Halem.

Halem, who lives in Kent, launched the glass program at Kent State University in 1969, retiring in 1998. His works are included in the collections of, among others, the Cleveland Museum of Art, the Detroit Institute of Arts, the Corning Museum of Glass and the Museum of Decorative Arts in Prague in the Czech Republic.

His art is "ordinary glass boxes filled with extraordinary things," as the reviewer of a 2015 Halem show in Tucson, Arizona put it.

Halem struck a chord with Belkin from the start.

"Mike and I seemed to enjoy each other's company from the beginning," Halem says. "I enjoyed his camaraderie and the warmth of his home. I was always flattered when he would ask me for advice on works he was considering buying. I always offered my subjective opinion and he always respected what I had to say. Although it was his interest in glass that brought us together, the friendship extended beyond that. Once in a while I would get a call and he would ask if I wanted to go to a basketball game or an Indians game. We are close in age and shared common experiences growing up. I think we always enjoyed talking popular music—which we both loved—and I was always grateful when he could get me tickets to something

The innards of this Henry Halem piece seem to push against its frame.

memorable like a Bob Dylan concert or when we were in California together and he got me and my friends backstage passes to a memorable rock concert."

In the same fashion as Weinberg, Halem advised Belkin on what art glass to buy, particularly work by Stanislav Libensky and Jaroslava Brychtova, a Czech couple known for its glass sculptures and their purity of color.

"I remember once I told him about a Libensky/Brychtova glass exhibition being held at the Heller Gallery," Halem says. "At the time, he did not know anything about their work or any of the Czech artists. He said, let's go, and we jumped on a plane and went to the show. I think it was the first time he saw their sculptural work and was totally in awe. If memory serves me correctly, he purchased two pieces from that show."

Mike and Annie Belkin with a prized Libensky/Brychtova.

There also were more personal connections. "It was always great fun to be invited to his and Annie's Halloween party and dress up in some silly costume," Halem says. "There were many memorable dinners and great wine, and best of all, Mike always picked up the check. What a guy."

Weinberg, too, is a fan of Libensky/Brychtova, and a distinctive craftsman himself. Both he and Halem claim to have been the persuasive influence that led Belkin to buy his first work by the Czech glass legends.

In a conversation from his home in Providence, Rhode Island, Weinberg's ex-wife and spokesperson, Sharon Oleksiak, said, "Mike wasn't sure if he really liked it and Steven convinced him to buy it and kept telling Mike he'd buy it back from him at any time if he didn't like it. And then it ended up being one of Mike's favorite pieces."

Steven Weinberg

Weinberg, a student of Dale Chihuly's, has twice been awarded a National Endowment for the Arts grant. He is known for his geometrically oriented crystal work.

The Belkins helped celebrate Weinberg's 46th birthday at a pig roast Oleksiak arranged on a farm in Rhode Island. Belkin is godfather to Weinberg's son, Charles.

Beyond the support of friendship, Belkin understood what it meant to throw support behind an artist, Oleksiak says. "He really, truly was what a patron of the arts should be. He really got behind the artist ... if Steven was struggling for money, he could say, 'Hey, Mike, want to buy a piece?' "

They would talk it over, settling on the right artwork, "but Mike also understood the economics of keeping a glass studio running and an artist keeping his family fed. He wasn't just a one-shot deal. When he got behind an artist, he got behind them in a steady way."

As a result of that constancy and level of knowledge, occupying a spot in the Belkin collection is a distinction.

"If it was a Belkin kind of piece, that was often good public relations, because collectors are kind of like pack animals," says Oleksiak. "There's a leader that buys an artist, so all of them want to buy that artist, and it certainly helped Steven's career to be in the Belkin collection."

Steven Weinberg's work plays off layering and mass.

That Belkin and Weinberg were both self-made deepened their bond.

"Mike was someone Steven could ask business questions of," says Oleksiak. "There are a lot of artists who really are not good business-people, and I don't know how they keep their studios open. Steven always was a good businessperson, too, I think. I think that (explains) some of the respect he has for Mike Belkin."

William Carlson's pieces are massive constructions of glass, metal and marble.

William Carlson

Like Weinberg, Carlson goes deep with Belkin on the personal level.

A 1973 Cleveland Institute of Art graduate, Carlson spent 1976 to 2003 as head of the art department at the University of Illinois, Urbana-Champaign. In the '80s, when Carlson was trying to build a studio at the University of Illinois, Belkin organized a program in which he would buy Carlson pieces and then sell some to galleries, giving Carlson a structure and income.

Carlson says that while the artistry of a piece is Belkin's primary consideration, he "also has a strong eye on the investment he's putting in; he knows the secondary market of glass … he understands that the work will end up in other places and will be seen by other folks." Belkin doesn't want to put his money into something "that doesn't have some longevity to it. And the longevity with art is the historical reference to where it fits into a time or place.

"He was very good to support me along the way by getting my pieces," says Carlson. "I gave him a great price, but he also was very beneficial in trying to keep my career going and he appreciated what was unique in my approach to the glass."

In 2003, Carlson moved to the University of Miami to become chair of the department of art and art history. It was in southern Florida that the couples became especially close, as Bill and Annie frequently visited Mike and Annie in Key Biscayne.

On a more down-to-earth note, Belkin appointed Carlson a judge at several of the Great American Rib Cook-Off festivals. Carlson would bring his kids along, and the families had fun together. Carlson, who lives in western Massachusetts, likes ribs—"though I was not necessarily qualified to be a judge."

Eventually, the Belkins' son, Sam, attended the University of Miami as an undergraduate and took glass classes from Carlson (Sam matriculated in 2012, his major anthropology, his minor glass blowing). Sam calls Carlson "Uncle Billy."

When a close friend from college came to visit, "for the first time, he saw where I grew up, and he finally understood me," Sam says. The friend recognized that Sam had grown "up in this intensely modern and cool house with an extremely loving and warm family ... You see the art around here, and it's very modern, but there are all these different, homey and warm things."

William Carlson, left, and Mike Belkin behind Sam Belkin.
Steven Weinberg is in front.

Chapter 11

In It for the Long Haul

I had a long, long list
Of everything I wanted to do ...

Michael Stanley ~ *The Real Thing*

Even when he's working or engaging in serious personal interests, Mike Belkin has a knack for play. Whether he is pairing socks, assembling rock 'n' roll lineups, collecting art, or selling tchotchkes, he loves what he does, and his energy is infectious. His immediate family is top of mind, too. It is his pride and his joy and his purpose. Mike Belkin takes care of his own.

Shortly after Belkin married the former Annie Elledge on Christmas Eve 1988, his first-born, Michael, who was 29 at the time, wished his father the best for his evolving family. Dated December 21, 1989, a handwritten card, framed and hung on a wall leading upstairs, says, "Dear Dad, I love and respect you so very much – this really says it all. I hope your next son is as fortunate as I am! Love, Michael."

On January 26, 1990, Annie Belkin gave birth to Belkin's next son, Samuel Ray Belkin.

Michael knew his father's baby boy was important to both Mike and Annie, and he was happy for them. "It was nice, because there hadn't been any new blood in the family for some time," he says. (Michael and his sister, Lisa, would each have two children of their own.)

A Different Drummer

At 27, Sam already has quite a résumé. He earned a bachelor of arts degree in anthropology from the University of Miami in 2012, with a minor in glass blowing. He earned a master's degree in sociocultural anthropology from Northern Arizona University in 2014,

and expects to complete his Ph.D. in sociology at the University of Leicester in England in 2020. An adjunct professor at both Lake Erie College in Painesville and Lakeland Community College in Kirtland, he teaches anthropology, sociology, sports sciences and sports management.

"It's been clear I've always done my own thing," says Sam, who never was interested in the rock 'n' roll business.

Mike Belkin socializes with his grandson, Jack, Michael's son.

Sam and Mike Belkin visit the Colosseum in Rome.

Yet his strong sense of purpose, that individualistic drive, is something he got from his father, he says.

Sam notes that just as he selected his own career path distinct from his dad's, so too did Mike when he moved away from the clothing business. "He followed his passion, his interest, and for him, it was a great success," says Sam.

Father and youngest son, who clearly adore and support each other, differ in other ways, too. Where Mike Belkin loves and played baseball and basketball, Sam took to swimming, a more individual endeavor. Where Mike loves to run many things simultaneously, Sam's passion is more singular and focused. As a teacher in the classroom, boardroom or online, he is driven by his respect for knowledge, which he views as a permanent investment. "Knowledge is something that can't be taken away," he says.

Even though Sam's interests diverge from brother Michael's, they share something more important: a strong respect and love for each other. As Michael says wryly, "If we were to sit down and I were to ask him about a song on the radio, or a player the Indians just signed, he would have no idea what I was talking about. And if he were to tell me about some of the things that he's interested in, that he teaches in class, my eyes would glaze over in equal form."

As for his relationship with his father, Sam says he continues to seek advice from his father on how to handle sticky situations, particularly within the social hierarchies that permeate academia. Mike also helped him with contract law when he was managing a fashion model while attending the University of Miami as an undergraduate.

"What he's taught me is life stuff, if that makes sense," Sam says. Call the elder Belkin's teachings lessons in life management. Sam gets those in equal measure from his mother Annie, too.

His family "is the same as pretty much any American family," Sam says. "We are headstrong, we love and respect each other, and take care of one another first."

Full of Surprises

As the only daughter of a rock star dad, Lisa Belkin enjoys a different but equally positive relationship with her father. Besides his lack of pretensions, Lisa is quick to list other attributes. "He is generous, caring, thoughtful, funny," she says. "All my friends have always thought he was really handsome, and still do. When we're out and people would ask if he was Mike Belkin from Belkin Productions, he was always very gracious. He was polite to everybody, which to me is the ultimate example of someone who is down to earth."

A graduate of Ohio State University and Cleveland State University's Marshall College of Law, Lisa worked part-time in the legal and accounting departments of Belkin Productions, and now works in accounting at Pinnacle.

She enjoyed growing up in the '70s. That's when she began going to rock shows. Unlike for most peers her age, these outings were family affairs: "As a family, we went to a lot of shows, and Michael and I would want to go, so the babysitter got to go, too."

In general, Belkin was not overly protective. "My mother covered that; he didn't have to be," says Lisa. At the same time, Belkin was inclusive, giving his kids plenty of rope and often even joined in their play. Lisa fondly recalls how he made a point to include her and Michael in backyard baseball, and on trips

Lisa Belkin with her dad.

like a safari in Kenya the three went on when Michael was 18, Lisa 16.

Witty repartee was also a norm. "He liked to tease a lot, and he still does. When I was a little girl—all of my life he told me that—he would say you throw like a girl, and I was so insulted," she says. "One day, when I must have been in high school, I said, 'I am a girl, that's why I throw like a girl.' He laughed."

When it comes to giving enough rope, another Belkin story speaks to his management style, even within family. It also attests to his love of the unusual, in this case, an exotic British car. Michael and Lisa—both lean and athletic—were in their early teens, when Michael had baseball aspirations.

"My father had this car that was a Jensen, some kind of small two-seater sports car, and my brother and I had to squish in the front seat together," Lisa recalls. "My brother was talking repeatedly about trying chewing tobacco, so my father stopped and got some and said to my brother, now we're back in the car, don't swallow your saliva.

"So, as the little sister, I said, Dad, he just swallowed, I just saw him swallow. My brother says, Stop the car, I got to throw up. So my

LINER NOTES.................

So, Where's the Picture... Not?

One show stands out for Lisa, and not for the music. The date was June 26, 1971, and the star was David Cassidy, presented at Public Hall. Lisa was thrilled to meet one of her idols, whose poster, along with one of the Osmond Brothers, hung on a wall in her bedroom on Bridgeton Road.

Lisa still wishes she had a very special memento from that night, however.

"My father was bringing David Cassidy into town so I went to the concert and beforehand I got to meet him and my father was going to take our picture," she recalls. "David Cassidy had me sit on a chair with him for my father to take the picture and I never saw the picture. I have asked and asked, and he said that was back in the days of film, and there was either no film in the camera or he messed up in the process. I have told him I have not forgiven him for that, and we laugh about it now."

father pulls over to the side of the road, Michael opens the car door, and throws up. My father didn't have a towel; he said, I only have a pair of clean underwear, and he took them out of his suitcase—he had picked us up at my mom's house for a visit on his way back from the airport—and he wiped off the car."

Reminded of this event, Belkin chuckles at the story but scowls at the memory of the car. The last straw was a window that wouldn't roll up, with the temperature below zero.

Her father "taught me respect, generosity, thoughtfulness, and how to enjoy things," says Lisa. "He also taught me there are different types of people in the world. He's an idea guy, very good at thinking outside the box. He came up with the Concert Club, the World Series of Rock. I'm just not a creative thinker. He is."

The Belkin School of Rock

While Mike Belkin continues to manage Michael Stanley and Donnie Iris and the Cruisers and arrange festivals for Live Nation, son Michael books bands in venues spanning clubs and arenas. He came up through the ranks at Belkin Productions, joining it in January 1983, two weeks after graduating from Ohio State University with a business degree. Driven, like his dad, he's conscious of carrying on in his father's profession. Tolerant and protective of each other, the two are extremely close.

While Michael was in college—first at Indiana University, later at OSU—he met some of the women his father dated. "I never sit in judgment of anybody else's decisions or anything like that," he says. "He dated people. I liked them. He lived with people. I liked them. He married somebody. I love her. I never got involved in whatever his things were outside of work. My only interest was the concerts ... I had a phenomenal work ethic, I was an animal and I went for it, and it worked out. But outside of the office, I didn't get involved in too much else."

What got him a Belkin Productions job? DNA, he jokes.

Michael Belkin, left, with Mike.

Michael interned at Belkin Productions all through his years at Beachwood High School. He began as a marketing assistant, and helped out one of his mentors, Barry Gabel, with the Belkin Concert Club. (His other key role models were his father, his Uncle Jules, Stacey Harper and Wendy Stein.)

His formal entry into the rock business was, one might say, vague. *Plain Dealer* rock writer Jane Scott reported that "Michael Belkin Jr." had been hired as a "trouble shooter," which meant to him that "it was pretty clear that I didn't have a lot of skills and that … my father and uncle didn't know what to do with me, so I was on the payroll with a little bit of uncertainty as to what this kid was capable of doing."

During his first year, he counted and tracked tickets. The following year, he was tapped to fill a production position.

In early 1984, Wendy Stein married and left town, creating an opening in production. "Somebody came to me and said, you're going to be, like, Stacey's underling, her apprentice," Michael says. Apprehensive, he sought his father's advice. Belkin broke down the position for him and made the job sound manageable.

"He said, you know, what's to do? It's all on paper. You look at the rider, and you call stagehands, you need four riggers and truck loaders and you look at how much electrical power you need, and that's what you get. He said it's all in black and white, and I'm embarrassed to say it was kind of a revelation and relief. He helped put me at ease."

After some seven years as a production manager—"Stacey was and even is to this day the senior and far superior production representative"—Michael took on yet another duty, booking smaller bands into smaller rooms like Peabody's DownUnder, the Agora and the Phantasy Nightclub in the Cleveland area, Boga-

Lisa and Michael Belkin flank their father.

rt's in Cincinnati, Newport Music Hall in Columbus, and the Orbit Room in Grand Rapids, Michigan. Those bookings, added onto the larger shows Jules Belkin continued to book, were not very profitable until Belkin Productions bought its first venue, the Odeon Concert Club, in 1994, Michael says.

But the club activity certainly extended the Belkin Productions brand, and there were other benefits. "It was everything except profitable," Michael says. "It was ancillary, supplemental, and it wasn't profitable. But it did have a couple of positive outcomes. One was that we were able to establish relationships with the artists earlier in their career and also it enabled us to become profitable in that sector when we purchased the Odeon in the Flats."

The Odeon venture also elevated Michael into select rock business company. "It enabled me personally to build relationships with professionals in the industry just starting out like myself who are now the senior staffers at the most important talent agencies in the world," says Michael, now senior vice president of Live Nation.

Belkin Productions was an easy place at which to be employed, though the work was hard. "I didn't mind the hours, driving home from a show in Columbus and getting home at 2 o'clock and being in the office the next day at 9:30, none of that bothered me," Michael says. "I liked organizing the shows. I've always been an organized person, so it actually was a job that I was strangely enough suited for … making sure the pieces fit. And for booking, I liked having a knack for trying to be intuitive about how many tickets a group would sell, what was the best building for the show, what were the appropriate ticket prices."

From his father, he says, he learned his work ethic, the fundamentals of the rock business, and a refusal to settle for the half-baked. But Mike also had his own prescient way of viewing the world.

To Michael, his dad "has a sense that he's always the first to see around the corner.

"I'm not necessarily that way, but I think it's part of what has enabled him to be a success at Belkin Productions. He was never really satisfied, he always wanted to continue to find something new and grow what he had and see what else is out there."

And, Michael notes, Belkin has always "had an eye for the presentation end of it."

Belkin also was willing to take an idea to market even if it ultimately fizzled.

For example, for a few years in the '70s, Belkin Productions published the Midwest Report, a kind of tip sheet that was essentially a compilation of radio station data. It didn't last, but it showed that Belkin wasn't scared to try something new, and was in tune with the times.

"It was an era that was exciting because we were obviously a significant concert promoter in artist representation and had a record label, and then we also tried the publishing element," says Michael. "The moral of the story is that he wasn't scared to put his toe in the water to try something we really hadn't done previously."

A Lasting Chemistry

Fond memories and today's joys seem to play on a screen inside her head when Annie Belkin speaks of her husband. Fittingly, she met

Mike Belkin on a plane, kindling a love that continues to be anything but earthbound.

It was sometime in the mid-'80s when Annie, a flight attendant on Midway Airlines, met Belkin on an early-morning flight from Chicago to Cleveland. Not too many passengers were aboard, and he was the only one in first class, which she was working. Belkin kept staring at her, making her uncomfortable, so Annie went to the back of the airplane to hang out with

Annie Belkin at home.

the other attendants. Eventually, Belkin went back there to talk to her, and she wound up joining him at the front of the plane, and "sat on the chair arm next to his seat and we talked for a while."

Belkin told her he'd come in from New Orleans, mentioning that he managed Mason Ruffner, whom he'd spent time with in the Crescent City. He was on his way to a meeting. Annie told him she had a three-hour layover and then did something she'd never done before: gave a passenger her telephone number. She was in her 20s. He was in his 50s.

The two didn't connect that day. There were no cell phones then, so making connections could be problematic. Belkin lived in Cleveland, and Annie lived in the Little Italy section of Chicago's Near West Side. They were more than curious about each other, however,

Annie and Mike Belkin with their son, Sam.

so some three months after their initial encounter, they finally found the time—and quite the place.

"He flew into Chicago and he was staying at the Ritz. I met him in the lobby. There was a chair right in front of the elevator and this guy comes off, he's dressed all in white—super-tan, like super-tan—and tall," says Annie. "Had he not known who I was, he could have walked right by me. I'm sitting down looking up and there's this guy. That was him. We went to dinner."

They dated for a few years. They dated other people, too, and Annie got engaged to one of them. However, that fiancé did not turn out to be Mr. Right.

"We had a long-distance relationship for a while," she says of Belkin. "When we first started going out, I told him, because I'd been with this other guy for six years, I wanted to get married and I wanted to have a kid, and if he didn't want to, if that wasn't part of his plan, that was OK, we'd go out and have a good time." She made it clear from the beginning that she was looking for a form of permanence, for family. But she also acknowledged that Belkin "had been married, he'd already had two kids, he'd already lived that life.

"I wasn't sure that was something he would like to do again, but he made it clear that he was willing, that was something he would do with me, that was a whole different experience," she says. "It was a different time, 20 years later."

Annie would have liked more kids with Belkin, but says the age gap worried Mike. He was afraid he'd saddle her with a brood of "children with no father to take care of them." So they stopped after Sam. "Instead of six boys, I got one perfect one," she says, laughing.

"When we got married, some of his closer and older friends were like, oh, she's just a flash in the pan, she's not going to last," she says. "I'm kind of an old-fashioned girl. I married him because I loved him, I married for life. So stick it to them." She laughs. "We made it."

They are each other's best friends, and now that Sam is on his own, their household is "just the two of us again. We're very lucky that we still like each other, and not only love each other. There's a lot of mutual respect."

Part of Annie's respect is due to Mike's commitment to remain occupied. "He's always been busy," says Annie. "He's always worked.

Annie and Mike Belkin on vacation.

He works hard and he loves what he does, no matter what it is, whether it's the music business or it's Pinnacle or selling a pen or a T-shirt to somebody and making 50 cents, it doesn't really matter. He enjoys the sale."

And they enjoy where they live, the art they live with, the company they keep, the organizations to which they contribute, like the Cleveland Metroparks Zoo, Park Synagogue, the Cleveland Museum of Art, the Akron Art Museum, the Rock and Roll Hall of Fame, and the Corning Museum of Glass.

All Annie wants is to spend more time with her husband, so all she asks of him is to "just leave a little in the tank" for her when he gets home. Time is the issue, not love. As she realized when Belkin offered her a wonderful way out of a very bad relationship, "he loves me beyond beyond." Annie tears up.

Range Boss

It is fortunate that Mike Belkin's an early riser. There's so much to do and not enough hours in the day.

There are old friends to catch up with, new musical talents to consider managing. There are magazines stacked on the table, but there's never enough time to read. There are household matters to address.

Boredom has never threatened Belkin. If he isn't preoccupied by the day-to-day and the close-to-home, he's attending a business conference or traveling. The man always seems to be on the move.

Stylish, urbane, patriotic, he's a tease, he's as quick to laugh as to cry, and he's a jokester who will tell you something so outrageous you almost believe him, except he can't maintain the deadpan quite long enough.

Belkin is still the boy who took to the "stage" in his aunts' parlor decades ago, foreshadowing early on that he was destined to make a distinctive theatrical mark. He's the man who put together lineups

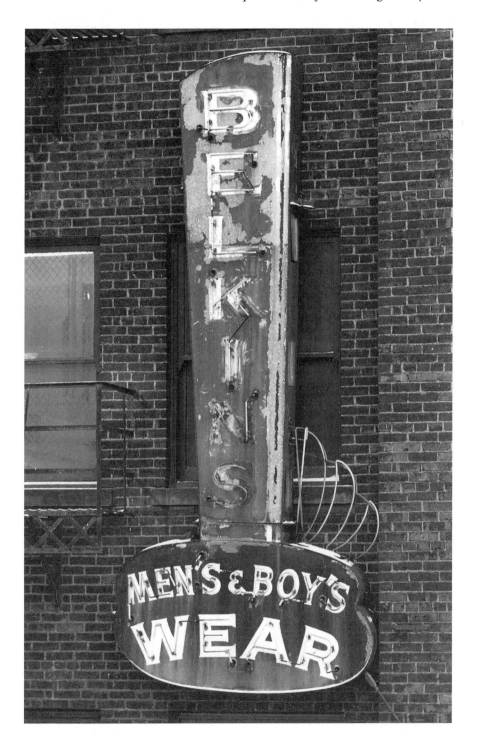

of rock 'n' roll bands that drew more people to downtown Cleveland than the city's professional sports teams.

Belkin is a connoisseur of art, an inveterate traveler, a confidant, a *bon vivant*, a talented athlete who applauds more talented athletes. He'll take a gamble, give advice, and put his considerable trust and resources behind anyone he believes in.

Mike Belkin is above all game, bringing spirit, heart and competitiveness to all his enterprises. As his son Michael says, he can see around that corner and capitalize on what he finds there. A sportsman to his marrow, he embodies the best qualities of elite athletes on the field. So, naturally, he likes to win. As Mike says, "I don't saddle up to come in second."

Encore

By Mike Belkin

Knowing my life better than anybody else, I felt—good, bad and otherwise—that it may be of interest to others, too. I wanted this book to tell just how fortunate I am. Many people have asked me about my life, and I felt this would be the best way to respond to them.

What I liked best about creating this book and what I liked least are the same: Carlo Wolff asking me all the time, when did that happen? My answer was always the same: How am I supposed to remember a date from 40 or 50 years ago?

My favorite stories, which I have related numerous times, tend to involve the bands I manage. Touring with the James Gang was a blast and getting into trouble with Michael Stanley and Donnie Iris and the Cruisers is an ongoing pleasure.

Associating with creative individuals, in music and in art, continues to bring me joy. Going to work at Pinnacle, where my wife, Annie, my grandson, Kevin, my daughter, Lisa, and my right-hand man, Todd Mullins, also work, rewards me daily. Above all, my family—Annie, Lisa, and my sons, Michael and Sam—gets me through thick and thin with their love.

I love my life.

Mike Belkin
Cleveland, Ohio
May 2017

Acknowledgements

Carlo Wolff

First of all, I want to thank Mike Belkin's gracious family: His wife, Annie, and his children, Michael, Lisa and Sam. Their insights into this man of many interests flesh out the verbal picture I have attempted to paint.

I also want to thank the following for contributing to and sharpening that picture: Mark Avsec, Mike Butz, William Carlson, Jim Fox, Barry Gabel, Henry Halem, the internet, Donnie Iris, Chris Jacobs, Michael Miller, Michael Norman, Pat Randle, Mike's former wife Sue Rubin, Paul Stankard, Michael Stanley, Steven Weinberg, and John S. Wilson.

On a more personal note, I want to thank the versatile Ron Hill (aided by Jaime Lombardo and James O'Hare of Act 3), without whom I could not have completed this; my wife, the multitalented Karen Sandstrom; and, of course, Mike Belkin himself. Mike jumpstarted this venture nearly two years ago and has been the soul of patience, not to mention the source of great stories.

Acknowledgements

Mike Belkin

Were it not for the following individuals this book would not have happened.

First and foremost, thank you to my mother, Pola (Mom), and my father, Sam (Dad), who were always there when I needed them, and God knows there were a multitude of times. Whether it would be financial, or, more importantly, just their love, they never failed me. The love that they gave to me I have passed on to my three incredible children, whom I will love and continue to kiss every time I see them. Yes, we are a kissing family.

Thanks to my first wife, Sue, who to this day I kiss on all family occasions, whether it be birthdays or holidays. Thank you, Stan (Sue's husband), and to the "Love of My Life," Annie, for understanding.

I have been very fortunate to have managed the careers of Michael Stanley, Donnie Iris, and Mark Avsec; I am extremely grateful that these business partnerships have evolved into deep, life-long friendships. I also thank Mason Ruffner, Jimmy Fox, Dale Peters, Joe Walsh and the late Doug Sahm, talented musicians who allowed me the honor of managing their careers, as well.

I also need to thank the incredible artists who have taught me about glass art. Thank you to Paul Stankard, Bill Carlson, Henry Halem and Steven Weinberg.

The process of this book took on a life of its own. Thanks for the many three- and four-hour conversations with my biographer, Carlo Wolff, who was typing while I was talking, and to Ron Hill, a new friend of mine, who was a pleasure to work with, in addition to being a brilliant illustrator.

My wife Annie has been an unbelievable person, always taking care of me, especially when I have needed medical care, after "totaling" two cars. She keeps me healthy; thank you.

Thank you to Michael, my first-born, who has taken over what I did, promoting concerts and managing musicians.

Much love and thanks to Lisa, my second-born, who made me a very happy father. Lisa, an attorney, decided that was not her love and now is treasurer of Pinnacle Marketing.

Last but certainly not least, thank you to Sam, my third-born, who turned out to be the "brains" of the family—a college professor— which I tease him about.

Photo Credits and Song Lyrics

All photos, unless otherwise credited, are from Mike Belkin's family collections and archives.

Many family photos were taken by Annie Belkin.

The following photos appear with the permission of Bob Ferrell (pages xix, 67, 107, 117, 122, 165); Janet Macoska (page 125); Robert Muller (page 143); and Frankie Valli (pages ix, x).

Many of the ads are used permission of Scene magazine.

All of the song lyrics used on the first page of each chapter are by creators that Mike Belkin managed, represented or produced.

Album covers and the aforementioned song lyrics, and in certain cases other content, were used for the necessary and transformative purpose of reporting or commenting on Mike's life and the artists he managed (as well as the songs they wrote). Care was taken so that the portion used of such content (including album covers and song lyrics) was reasonable in light of the purpose of this book. Use of such content comports with the guidelines of 17 U.S.C. § 107.

About Carlo Wolff

Carlo Wolff is a publishing veteran specializing in music criticism, features, hospitality and travel journalism, corporate content writing and copy editing. A regular contributor to the jazz magazine, *DownBeat*, he is the author of *Cleveland Rock & Roll Memories* (Gray & Co., 2006) and co-writer, with Eric Olsen and Paul Verna, of *The Encyclopedia of Record Producers* (Billboard, 1999). Wolff has been a reporter for and editor of both mainstream and alternative daily and weekly newspapers, and a review of his is contained in "Killed," a compilation of censored journalism published by The Nation Books. A native of Dallas, Texas, Wolff grew up in Columbus, Ohio, and attended schools in the Boston area, earning a bachelor of fine arts degree with an English major from Boston University. Before he moved to Cleveland in 1986, he lived in Burlington, Vermont and Albany, New York. Wolff lives in suburban Cleveland with his wife, two dogs and a cat.

About Mike Belkin

Mike Belkin was half of Belkin Productions, the premier rock music promoter in Cleveland and the Midwest, for four decades starting in the mid 1960s. After playing professional baseball for the Milwaukee Braves farm system in Texas, Belkin returned to his hometown to become a show promoter (The World Series of Rock shows in the 1970s set outdoor venue records that still stand), band manager (he still manages Midwest rock icons Michael Stanley and Donnie Iris), and a record producer ("Play That Funky Music" which still earns very robust royalties). He is currently owner and president of Pinnacle Marketing, a professional sports licensing firm. Belkin is also a respected art glass authority, co-founding the Art Alliance for Contemporary Glass, and a fellow of the Corning Museum of Glass. In 2012, Belkin and his wife Annie donated 64 pieces to a permanent contemporary glass collection at the Akron Museum of Art. In 2015, Belkin and his brother Jules were honored with the Martha Joseph Cleveland Arts Prize. Belkin and his wife live in a sprawling home filled with art in rural Northeast Ohio.